D0849421

WHAT PAUL REALLY SAID ABOUT WOMEN

WHAT PAUL REALLY SAID ABOUT WOMEN

John Temple Bristow

1817

Harper & Row, Publishers, San Francisco

Cambridge, Hagerstown, New York, Philadelphia, Washington
London, Mexico City, São Paulo, Singapore, Sydney

Library of Congress Cataloging-in-Publication Data

Bristow, John Temple.
  What Paul really said about women.

1. Paul, the Apostle, Saint—Views on women.
2. Woman (Christian theology)—Biblical teaching.
3. Bible. N. T. Epistles of Paul—Criticism,
interpretation, etc. I. Title.
BS2655.W5B73 1988   227'.083054   87-46200
ISBN 0-06-061059-4

88 89 90 91 92 HC 10 9 8 7 6 5 4 3 2 1

To my wife, Christy, and to the members of the Lake City Christian Church (Disciples of Christ) in Seattle, of whom Saint Paul might have written that there is "neither male nor female, for you are all one in Christ Jesus," and added as well "neither black nor white, neither young nor old, neither rich nor poor."

CONTENTS

Preface: Surprises That Led to the Writing of This Book

In many ways we humans are too complex for our own understanding, especially in the area of the relationship between the sexes. That's a mystery as old as Eden—and the experience in Eden did not help solve the mystery, either.

As a youth, I, along with most of my generation, fell heir to the traditional interpretation of what the apostle Paul declared to be true about women. We also fell heir to the traditional double standard for the sexes. Neither of these ways of thinking, taken alone, made much sense. Taken together, they made even less sense.

For example, we were taught that women, according to the good apostle Paul, are more prone to fall when tempted than are men. After all, just look at the example of Eve. On the other hand, we were taught that women, according to the double standard, are responsible for upholding sexual virtues. After all, boys will be boys, but girls must be ladies and must tell the boys when to behave. Now, one may wonder, if females are less resistent to temptation, why it is they who must tell males when enough is enough?

We were also taught that women, according to Paul, are to obey their husbands and to be subject to male leadership. On the other hand, we were taught that women, according to the double standard, have the ultimate position of leadership. After all, "the hand that rocks the cradle rules the world." One may wonder, if women are less fit leaders than men, how mothers can teach their sons to be good leaders?

Since that time, modern psychology has gathered more and more data and has discovered that previous data were in error about women. These new data confirm what ordinary observation reveals, that both women and men are able to learn, reason, develop skills, and demonstrate creativity. And as the distinction between what used to be regarded as men's roles and women's roles has slowly faded, so has the double standard (replaced, some may argue, with few or no standards at all). And where has all this change left the apostle Paul?

Many people who believe in the authority of Scripture have not been willing to abandon what they regard as the divine plan for men and women, no matter what changes might be taking place in the world. They choose to remain faithful to the traditional understanding of Paul's teachings.

Other people who are determined to live by the truth as they understand it, regardless of its origin, have raised serious questions regarding the authority of Paul's words. Many such thoughtful people have concluded that Paul was terribly inconsistent. He affirmed that in Christ there is neither male nor female, yet he also insisted that wives be subject to their husbands and that women are morally weaker than men. He seemed to accept the idea of women speaking during worship in the congregation in Corinth, yet he told Timothy that women were to remain quiet in church.

Perhaps Paul was torn between the ideal and the realities of his time. Perhaps he compromised the gospel in order not to upset the social structures of his age. Perhaps Paul could not escape his own background and culture. Or perhaps Paul gave a good line in public, but in private revealed his own disdain regarding women.

As a pastor, I have been continually confronted with the issue of sexual equality versus the teachings of Paul. Should women take their place alongside men in sharing leadership in the Church? Is the ideal marriage based on a model of partnership or patriarchy? What about the portions of Scripture that extol examples of women engaging in activities we have been taught are outside the sphere of women's work? Moreover, if Paul was wrong, how can we trust any part of the Bible?

Behind all of these important and sensitive questions lies an assumption: that our traditional understanding of what Paul wrote is accurate, and that this understanding is what Paul really intended to communicate. But what happens if our traditional understanding of what Paul wrote is all wrong?

I have always admired the intellectual courage of Albert Einstein. One time he was asked what led him to his fresh, new approach that was so different from the physics of Isaac Newton, and he replied, "I challenged an axiom." In a sense, I sought an answer to these questions about Paul's teachings by challenging another axiom: that what we think Paul meant is really what Paul intended us to think.

I began with Paul's letter to the church at Ephesus, in which he states that wives are to be subject to their husbands and that husbands are to be as a head to their wives. Now, Paul's letters are in Greek. Theoretically, if I took our English translation of his words and translated them back into Greek, my words should be similar to Paul's original words. But when I tried doing this, such was not the case, not at all! In reality, the words that Paul chose to use imply different ideas from those conveyed by the English words we use to translate his writings. In fact, our English words imply ideas that Paul deliberately avoided! If Paul had wanted to say what we think he said, then he would have chosen quite different words when he wrote.

So I began to explore these differences in meanings. And soon I made a remarkable discovery: far from being an advocate of the notion that men are superior to women, Paul was in fact the first great champion of sexual equality! With deeper appreciation I recalled a prayer from the seventeenth century by Thomas Fuller, who confessed, "Lord, this morning I read a chapter in the Bible, and therein observed a memorable passage whereof I never took notice before. Why now, and no sooner, did I see it? Formerly my eyes were as open, and the letters as legible. Is there not a thin veil laid over Thy Word, which is more rarified by reading, and at last wholly worn away? I see the oil of Thy Word will never leave increasing whilst any bring an empty barrel."

However, time and time again I would doubt my discoveries, so deeply ingrained in my thinking was the traditional interpretation of what Paul (rightly or wrongly) intended us to believe. Each time I would return to my notes and recheck each step of my investigation, and each time reaffirm this exciting discovery.

At last I was forced to banish all doubts. In truth, Paul carefully chose his words, deliberately avoiding those Greek terms that, if he had used them, would have communicated to his readers precisely what our English translations imply for us today.

But I could not understand how the traditional misunderstanding of Paul's teachings about women and marriage could have arisen. So I explored those attitudes that were characteristic of Greek and Jewish societies during the age of the apostles. And I found that Paul stood squarely opposed to such attitudes, proclaiming instead a new order of sexual equality within the Church and within the home. This apostle championed the value of women. And therein lies one of the greatest ironies of Christian history: the words of Paul (as translated), instead of communicating a clear message calling for sexual equality, have become the primary source of authority for the deprecation of women!

Then I explored the history of this conflict between Paul's idea of sexual equality and the attitudes among Greeks and Jews of his time. I learned how the conflict was finally settled when Greek philosophy infused Christian theology, and Paul's message was lost and his words used to promote what he opposed. Paul's words about women, sex, and marriage were interpreted from the viewpoint of the teachings of Aristotle and of Stoic philosophers, the viewpoint already held by Gentile converts to the faith. In effect, the words of Paul, the Christian apostle, had their meanings molded to conform to the thoughts of Aristotle, a pagan philosopher who lived five centuries before Paul! And still today, this same Greek philosophy is often preached from Christian pulpits, innocently assumed to be biblical theology.

These discoveries excited me. It was as if the veil described by Thomas Fuller had been lifted from my own eyes, and now

I could read afresh the urgent cry from Paul for churches to have women learn, to let them be leaders, to let them have the authority due them, to realize in practice the great truth that "there is neither male nor female . . . you are all one in Christ Jesus" (Gal. 3:28). I found that Paul presented a new and modern-sounding model for husbands and wives, one that offers a fresh quality to marital interaction.

Then I began to include these new insights in my preaching and teaching and to integrate them into the organizational life of the congregation. The responses to my efforts were quite mixed.

None of the warnings about what might happen if sexual equality were practiced in the Church proved to be justified. There was no decrease in the percentage of men among the active membership. There was no lessening of moral standards. And there was no decrease in trust in Scripture—in fact, some who had been offended at the traditional interpretation of Paul's writings about women and marriage began to demonstrate a keen interest in learning more about the Bible.

One woman, expressing her reaction to this new understanding of Paul's writings, received a number of nods of agreement when she said, "It affirms me as a woman." Another thoughtful young woman added, "I may not be able to make a good reply to those who quote Paul in an attempt to put women down, but now I have the mental assurance that their viewpoint is wrong."

Not all the members of the congregation greeted this new revelation of Paul's plea with enthusiasm. Thinking of the removal of barriers to women's serving in capacities previously reserved for men only, one older woman said, "You won't change the way of thinking I was brought up to believe, but it is good to see the younger women allowed the freedom to do what they want to do in the Church." One middle-aged man was not that flexible, however, declaring, "I don't care what the Bible says, I have my feelings!"

Visitors to the congregation offered mixed reactions. One

woman, when told of the basis for our openness toward sexual equality, exclaimed, "Oh, I believe it—that's what I've always thought Paul meant—but I've never seen it put into practice." One man declared, "It's a disgrace that the churches are so slow in doing what the world is wise enough to do already." But another man, following a worship service in which one of the leaders was a forty-year-old woman, approached her and announced that "it is not right to send a girl to do a man's job!" It was not until several minutes after he left that this woman figured out the term *girl* was aimed at her.

Another woman visited the congregation because she was told as a recovering alcoholic that she must learn to rely upon "a higher power." She did not believe in the existence of God, but her desperate search for sobriety led her to the Church's doors. Almost a year later, after she had worked through her doubts and had experienced a personal and precious sense of the living God, she told me, "If I had found, when I first came to this church, that women were regarded as second class, you would never have seen me again. I would have been out the door and never come back, and," she added, reflecting on her new faith, " I would have been unable to find what I did."

Best of all, women members have assumed more leadership responsibilities in response to this new insight into Paul's message. Given permission and encouragement, they have demonstrated very fine skills and a high level of energy, which have deeply enriched the church's program.

During my research into Paul's writings regarding women, sex, and marriage, I found a number of valuable resources. But I want to express special appreciation to Letha Scanzoni and Nancy Hardesty for their fine book *All We're Meant To Be*, and to Marcus Barth, author of the two-volume section of the Anchor Bible that deals with Ephesians (his footnotes alone served as a priceless treasure map to further study).

1. Where the Idea That Women Are Inferior to Men Really Began

A cartoon appeared in a Christian magazine about two decades ago, depicting Saint Paul arriving by boat on some distant shore, met by a group of women carrying placards that read "Unfair to Women," "Paul is a Male Chauvinist Pig," and the like. Paul looks sheepishly at this protest rally and says, "Heh, heh, I see you got my letter."

Throughout most of church history, the apostle Paul has held the reputation of being what one might call the Great Christian Male Chauvinist toward women. After all, did not Paul declare that women are not to speak in church? That husbands are to rule over their wives and wives are to obey their husbands? That women are more easily tempted than men? That women can be saved only by bearing children? That women are not to wear jewelry or nice clothing, or have their heads uncovered during worship?

Even such a scholar as Herbert J. Muller, writing on *Freedom in the Ancient World*, denounced the apostle Paul for deprecating women: "Although they [women] had fared well with Jesus, appearing as central figures in many of the gentlest parables and episodes of the Gospels, their degradation began with St. Paul. He took very literally the myth of Eve. While he remarked in passing that male and female were one in Christ Jesus, he taught more emphatically that on earth woman should be subject to her husband 'in everything,' as one who has been created for the sake of man. Even so, Paul did not really approve of her creation."[1]

This same condemnation of Paul is so firmly entrenched in the minds of most people who read the New Testament that the kindest thing one might hear of Paul's attitude toward women is that if Paul was not actually an out-and-out misogynist, a woman-hater, he was at least certainly inconsistent! On the one hand, Paul's writings about women have been cited throughout the centuries as authority for the notion that women are second-class citizens in the kingdom of God and the Church. On the other hand, Paul's great declaration in Gal. 3:28, "There is neither Jew nor Greek . . . neither male nor female, for you are all one in Christ Jesus," has been lifted up as equally authoritative by advocates of sexual equality. How can Paul's writings be used to defend these opposing points of view?

The beginning of this statement in Galatians deserves respectful attention. "There is neither Jew nor Greek"—these words are the central conviction of Paul's ministry, in his great ambition to bring together in the Church both Jewish and Gentile Christians. This dream was the heartbeat of his apostleship. Such a statement was certainly not written "in passing"! It would seem unlikely, then, that Paul would conclude this great declaration with the phrase "neither male nor female" if these words reflected only a slight sentiment for him, almost accidentally penned just before he wrote with firm conviction, "for you are all one in Christ Jesus."[2]

No, it was certainly not just "in passing" (as Muller contends) that Paul proclaimed "there is neither male nor female, for you are all one in Christ Jesus." In fact, if one dares to set aside the traditional certainty that Paul regarded women as inferior to men, and then if one also sets aside the implications inherent in the words used to translate Paul's writings, carefully studying only what Paul actually wrote, suddenly this apostle is revealed in a new light. He was not a believer in the inferiority of women. He did not advocate a secondary role for women in the Church. He did not teach some notion of a divine hierarchy, with husbands ruling over their wives.

Quite the contrary. Instead, the apostle Paul consistently championed the principle of sexual equality within the Church and the home. He carefully avoided those words in Greek that would connote meanings that—ironically—our modern English translations imply! He carefully selected his words in writing about women and marriage, challenging the social roles for women in his age and the philosophy and theology that defined these roles. And yet his words have been interpreted so as to defend the very roles he challenged!

How could such a transition be made, that Paul would become identified in the minds of so many as the arch-male-chauvinist of the Bible? It happened because those who first quoted Paul and interpreted his writings were themselves bearers of centuries of Greek philosophy. They understood Paul from the viewpoint of their own culture and customs. In a sense, they read Paul's words through the eyes of Aristotle. And in so doing, they established a traditional method of viewing Paul's insights from a perspective that was Greek rather than Jewish and pagan rather than Christian.

It All Began in Athens: The Greek Legacy of Disdain for Women

Athens was named after the lovely goddess of wisdom. How ironic that a system of philosophy that maintains that females are in all ways inferior to males should originate in a city named after a female deity who embodied wisdom!

Yet here in the capital of ancient Greece, in the brilliant minds of her philosophers and teachers, lies the source of the Western world's formalized conviction that women are inferior to men. Here was codified an attitude about females, a prejudice regarding women that Dr. Arthur Verral, a noted classical scholar, identified as "the radical disease, of which, more than anything else, ancient civilization perished."[3]

Perhaps this attitude was first expressed by the blind poet Homer, author of the *Iliad* and the *Odyssey*, as he sang of the struggles of distant heroes and how "each one gives law to his children and to his wives."[4] Or perhaps this attitude was first given social and religious sanction by Solon, called one of the Seven Wise Men of Greece, as he built a brothel in Athens and dedicated its profits to the erection of a temple to Aphrodite, the goddess of love.

But it was Socrates (c. 470–399 B.C.) who immortalized the Athenian disdain toward women. Often referring to women as "the weaker sex," he argued that being born a woman is a divine punishment, since a woman is halfway between a man and an animal.[5]

In some ways, Socrates seems at first glance to have been committed to the idea of sexual equality. In *The Republic*, Plato reports that Socrates advocated education and training for women as well as men, in order that women might share the same duties as men in this ideal society, including the duties of military service. Socrates based this idea on the observation that a female dog is as helpful to the shepherd as a male dog. And he rejected the notion that there are certain tasks that are woman's work and others that only men can do. "No practice or calling in the life of the city belongs to woman as woman," he taught, "or to man as man, but the various natures are dispensed among both sexes alike; by nature the woman has a share in all practices, and so has man, but in all, woman is rather weaker than man."[6]

However, even though Socrates felt that both men and women should perform all the various responsibilities of citizenship, he entertained no notions of equality between the sexes. "Do you know anything at all practiced among mankind," he asked, "in which in all these respects the male sex is not far better than the female?"[7]

One time Socrates humorously advised a young man, "By all means, get married. If you get a good wife, you will be happy. If you get a bad one, you will become a philosopher." But he argued that in the ideal society, marriage would be abandoned. "No one will deny," he was certain, "that it would be the greatest good to have women in common and children in common." It would be best for society for no man "to have a private wife of his own, and the children must be common too, and the parent shall not know the child nor the child its parent."[8] Opportunity for reproduction would be provided in a sort of lottery system, with much better odds secretly provided for those who were more apt to provide better offspring.

As restrictive as this model for society may seem by modern standards, it might well have been liberating for Athenian women. For in real life, respectable Greek wives led a completely secluded life. They took no part in public affairs, never appearing at meals or at social occasions. Recreation was severely limited for them, as were social contacts. Athenian men enjoyed outdoor sports and frequented the *agora*, the marketplace, which served as the center of city life and communication. Women were excluded from both. The ideal Athenian woman, according to Xenophon, a disciple of Socrates, was one who "might see as little as possible, hear as little as possible, and ask as little as possible."[9] Even conversation between husband and wife was neither valued nor expected. "Is there anyone to whom you entrust more serious matters than to your wife," Socrates asked Athenian men, "and is there anyone to whom you talk less?"[10]

The teachings of Socrates come down to us through his star pupil, Plato (c. 427–347 B.C.). And Plato's most distinguished disciple was Aristotle (384–322 B.C.), who left to the world a fascinating assortment of lectures on various subjects, including a collection on natural history. In his discourse on insects, he noted that a single bee will lead a vast swarm of bees to a new location, where they will industriously build a new nest and establish their complex society. And because the swarm follows one individual, Aristotle unquestioningly assumed that this single leader must be male, the "king bee." Centuries passed before naturalists corrected this false impression with objective observation. Only then was Aristotle's terminology changed to "queen bee."[11]

Why did Aristotle assume that the leader of a swarm must be male? Because he was firmly convinced that "the male is by nature fitter to command than the female." This is true, he taught, not just of bees, but of all creatures, especially humans. Moreover, he added, this "inequality is permanent."[12] Aristotle grudgingly admitted that there were those who taught how "in most constitutional states the citizens rule and are ruled in turns," but he insisted that applying this principle within households "is a mistake."[13]

It was "barbarian" in Aristotle's mind not to distinguish between a wife and a slave, but he disagreed with Socrates about the roles of the sexes. "The temperance of a man and of a woman or the courage and justice of a man and of a woman, are not, as Socrates maintained, the same," he declared. "The courage of a man is shown in commanding, of a woman in obeying."[14]

This difference between husband and wife, Aristotle explained, is like that of a man's soul and his body. The man is to his wife as a soul is to the physical body, meant to command and guide arms and legs with wisdom and intelligence. (Aristotle used this same analogy to defend the practice of slavery and define the relationship of master and slave.) Just as one's body, with its impulses and desires, should not rule his soul, so a wife should not rule her husband. And, he added, as a stern warning, the "equality of the two or rule of the inferior is always hurtful."[15]

Aristotle thus laid a lasting philosophical foundation for the notion that females are inferior to males. He formalized the practice of sexual discrimination and offered learned authority to the belief in sexual inequality. Centuries later, church leaders who themselves were a product of Greek culture and education interpreted Paul's writings from the perspective of Aristotelian philosophy, even to the point of assuming that when Paul wrote of the husband being head of the wife, he was simply restating

Aristotle's analogy of the husband being to his wife like one's soul to one's body. As will be seen, a careful reading of what Paul wrote demonstrates that this apostle was actually challenging Aristotle's idea instead of supporting it.

Demosthenes, who was born just one year earlier than Aristotle, was regarded as the greatest of Greek orators. He analyzed the roles of women in Athens in an oft-quoted statement: "We have courtesans for our pleasures, prostitutes [that is, young female slaves] for daily physical use, wives to bring up legitimate children and to be faithful stewards in household matters."[16]

Of these three options for Athenian women, the role of wife provided more security, but it also brought greater restrictions. These women were married at an early age to men whom they did not know. The arrangements were made for them, and a rich dowry was paid for this privilege. As wives, they received no education except in how to cook and spin and be modest and quiet. A friend of Xenophon's described his ideal marriage partner this way: "She was not yet fifteen when I introduced her to my house, and she had been brought up always under the strictest supervision; as far as could be managed, she had not been allowed to see anything, hear anything or ask any questions."[17]

Socrates admitted that his idea of having women trained to perform the same functions in society as men (however inferior the performance of women would be, naturally) was a radical departure from Athenian custom and would be very unlikely ever to win approval. He may have had in mind a statement made by Pericles, the principal ruler of Athens who strove to make that city the center of art and literature and architectural beauty (and who was responsible for the construction of the Parthenon, as well as other marvelous buildings). Pericles stated that it was the duty of an Athenian mother to live so retired a life that her name would never be mentioned among men, either for praise or for shame. Women in Athens never went out alone, never shared meals with men, and never entered into the life of the community. They led lives of greatest seclusion. The few Athenian women who were educated and could discuss current literature and philosophical thought were, for the most part, among the courtesans, upper-class prostitutes called *hetairai*. They attended lectures and were able to enter into intellectual discussions and debates with their clients.[18] Other, lower-class prostitutes and Greek matrons had no such educational opportunities.

In the generation after Aristotle, another Athenian philosopher named Zeno founded a school of thought that greatly influenced Greek and Roman society. He taught on a porch (which in Greek is *stoa*), and so his followers were called Stoics.

Zeno objected to the way men used women for their pleasure. However, his criticisms were not based on any concern for the rights or plight of women in Athenian society. Rather, he objected because men who became enamored with women might thereby be distracted from the study of philosophy. He taught that sexual intercourse is justified only when its purpose is procreation. All passions and pleasures are to be disdained by those who would truly pursue wisdom. Zeno's followers championed the value of asceticism and celibacy for the sake of higher goals, the search for truth.

In subsequent centuries the essence of that appeal was felt within the Christian church. The life of a celibate, it was supposed, is that most suited to a personal search for holiness in a corrupt and evil world. The finest and most devout men and women would forego sexual intimacy and marriage for the sake of higher spiritual goals.

The impact Stoic philosophy had on attitudes about women and sex might be illustrated in the person of Epictetus, a Stoic teacher in Rome until A.D. 90. He seemed reluctant to admit any possible good could be found within women, except perhaps that of physical beauty. "Do not admire your wife's beauty," he advised his pupils, "and you are not angry with the adulterer."[19] He taught that women, from the age of fourteen, think of nothing and aim at nothing but lying with men.[20] He constantly wrote of women as a temptation to men, how they lure "with softer voices" a young philosopher who is no match for a "pretty girl."[21] Other Stoic philosophers echoed these same sentiments regarding women.

The philosophers of Athens, then, bequeathed to the world a double indictment against womanhood. From the classic period, especially in the teachings of Aristotle, came the conviction that women are inferior to men. Therefore, women are to be commanded by men and used for the pleasure of men. Then, from the Stoic philosophers came the conviction that women are a distraction and temptation to men. Therefore, women are to be avoided by men who would thereby be free to pursue those qualities that make men superior. Both points of view underlie the traditional interpretations of the writings of Saint Paul regarding women and marriage.

The Spread of Athenian Philosophy to More Egalitarian Societies

Not all ancient societies shared this Athenian deprecation of the female sex, not even within the Greek-speaking world. The women in Sparta, in contrast to what has been called the "monogamous harem" of women in Athens, enjoyed considerable freedom and political responsibilities. The economic role of women in Sparta is reflected in the fact that at one time in that nation's history women owned two-thirds of the land.

Sparta, however, provided no philosophical heritage for the world. No Spartan teacher competed with the brilliant minds of Socrates, Aristotle, or Zeno. It was these who told the Western world what is the "best" role for women in society and in the home.

Egypt, even more than Sparta, demonstrated respect for its female citizens. Modern travelers in Egypt may observe how the colossal statues of Ramses II always dwarf the accompanying figures of his wife, and from this example of ancient Egyptian art they may conclude that male dominance was the norm in that society. But such was not the case.

Herodotus, who is called the father of history and who was a contemporary of Socrates, once traveled to Egypt, and there he was astonished at the way of life for Egyptian women. He wrote, "The Egyptians themselves in their manners and customs seem to have reversed the ordinary practices of mankind. For instance, women attend market and are employed in trade, while men stay at home and do the weaving."[22] A careful observation of the relics of middle-class households in ancient Egypt reveals a society that was quite equalitarian. It is little wonder that Herodotus was so shocked as he contrasted the activities of Egyptian women with the roles of Athenian women.

Women in Egypt had legal rights equal to those of men in the same social class. And women retained these rights as they entered into marriage. A middle-class woman might sit on a local tribunal and give judgment upon evidence against a defendant (one can hardly imagine this practice being accepted in Athens!). An Egyptian woman might inherit property and bequeath property. She might engage in real estate transactions, and she might use her land as security against a loan. She could witness legal documents and act upon her own in legal matters, without being obliged to have her husband cosign for her. She could buy, sell, or free slaves. She could adopt children. And she could press a suit in court (in fact, one eighteenth-century B.C. woman even sued her own father!).

In the exquisite art of Egyptian tombs, husbands and wives are often depicted with their arms around each other, or else holding hands. In scenes of family life, the wives are shown engaged in the same activities as their husbands and children. General respect for women is revealed in a maxim spoken by Ptahhotep of the Old Kingdom era: "Good speech is more hidden than the emerald, yet it may be found with maidservants at the grindstones."[23]

Egyptologist Barbara S. Lesko summarizes the role of women and their status within that culture:

Egyptian women were certainly not hesitant to appear in public, whether as merchants in the public market place or on the picket line supporting their husbands in the first recorded labor strike in history.

Indeed, when we take the trouble to examine Egyptian records, our understanding of the social condition of the ancient Egyptian women is a far cry from the "human misery" imagined by the classicist Edith Hamilton. The woman of ancient Greece was indeed in a pitiable plight, cloistered at home with her distaff while the men of her society filled the markets, theaters, stadia, and the law-courts. Nor were Greek husbands and wives found together at social events like private dinner parties; but the Egyptian couple went everywhere together, sharing life's trials and delights as respected and equal citizens in their secular and religious communities, enjoying equality under the law as well. Surely this was one of the glories of ancient Egypt.[24]

Egypt, however, provided no philosophical heritage for the world, no well-stated argument in favor of sexual equality to challenge the Greek degradation of women. It was the philosophers of Athens who told the world the "best" role for women in society and in the home.

During the middle of the fourth century B.C., Philip II of Macedon was conquering Greece; meanwhile, his son Alexander was in Athens being taught philosophy by Aristotle. After Philip was killed, Alexander began military campaigns that quickly brought the whole known world under his control.

The philosophy and culture of Athens seemed to be so superior to that of other nations, in the mind of Alexander at least, that he sought to enlighten his subjected peoples by inculcating Greek thought into their societies. This effort at converting differing cultures to the Greek way of life is called Hellenization. After Alexander died, his successors continued this process in the regions under their control, including Egypt and Judea.

Apparently, the state of sexual equality in Egyptian marriages persisted for some time, in spite of efforts to Hellenize that culture, judging from the disapproval expressed by a first-century B.C. Greek historian who wrote how the Egyptian wife "lords it over her husband as in the deed about the dower, the men agree to obey the wife in everything!"[25]

Women in the Age of Paul

Since Athens was the source of a philosophy that deprecated females, one would expect to find women enjoying greater degrees of freedom the farther west one traveled from Greece. And such was the case, in the time of Paul. A woman living in Rome, in contrast to one in Greece, was "her husband's comrade and cooperator," as one modern scholar observed.[26] She often accompanied her husband on outings and to social affairs. Roman women of the upper class were allowed to organize meetings and pursue academic studies. The spred of the Isis cult from Egypt affirmed these freedoms for women as they gathered together (without men) and learned to offer thanks to this goddess, who—they were taught to say—"gavest to women the same power as to men."[27]

But in spite of this relatively greater degree of freedom in Rome as compared to Athens, females were less valued than males. Girls might attend school as well as boys, but sons were favored. One ancient writer remarked that "even the rich man always exposes a daughter."[28] By this, he meant that even in a wealthy family the father often chooses to leave a newborn girl to die of exposure (a common means of Roman birth control). Roman women who were unmarried and who had no inherited wealth had to turn to prostitution in order to survive. In fact, a standard Latin term for prostitute, *meretrix*, means "she who earns," implying that this was the only way for a woman to receive an income.

Roman men tended to share the Greek view of women as objects of pleasure or else sources of temptation. This similarity of views is not remarkable, since Roman boys were taught by Greek tutors, who were themselves schooled in Greek philosophy, especially Stoic philosophy. Such teachers warned Roman men of the danger posed by a tempting woman, who might snare him through love and thereby distract him from attaining the higher goal of wisdom. One such philosopher, it is said, suffered from a fit of madness brought on by a love potion given him by his wife, and committed suicide. He was Lucretius (c. 96–55 B.C.), who taught that love made a man miserable. Love, he said, should be eradicated as soon as the first signs of its presence are felt. This is possible only if a man so inflicted will concentrate upon the faults of his beloved and reflect that physically one woman is like any other woman and none are to be desired over others.

Some other philosophers, however, held more moderate views regarding women and marriage. Notable among them was Plutarch (c. A.D. 46–120), a biographer of distinguished Greek and Roman personalities. He lived in the generation after Paul, and he taught Roman husbands that they were to be as mothers and fathers to their wives, treating them with kindness and goodwill. However, Plutarch's instructions were often two-sided, to the point of bordering on unintentional satyre. For example, he chastized those husbands who "labor to depress and degrade their wives, proud of the mastery and vaunting in domestic tyranny", and extolled those husbands who bestow upon their wives worth and dignity equal to that which they bestow upon their horses. He urged husbands "to sympathize in the sorrows and afflictions" of their wives, arguing that marriage is like the knitting of two cords into a knot "so the ligaments of conjugal society may be strengthened by the mutual interchange of kindness and affection", but he immediately carried this imagery of the marriage knot into an argument over why "the house and estate must be reputed the possession of the husband, although the woman brought the chiefest part." He compared a good marriage to the harmony within music, so that "all things are carried on with the harmonious consent and agreement of both parties", but he added that this harmony is based on the ability of the husband to manage their relationship. This management is not to be like that of a master over his slave, Plutarch insisted, but like that of the soul over the body, so that the authority of a man over his wife will be softened "with complaisance and kind requital of her loving submission."

The husband is responsible for his wife's education, Plutarch taught, to the point that she will say of him, "And you, my beloved husband, are my guide and tutor in philosophy beside, from whose instructions I at once improve the fruits of knowledge and the sweets of love." But is such education given to enable the wife to pursue new goals or some greater vocation? No, for according to Plutarch, a woman's "two great duties" are "to keep at home and be silent."

Married women, Plutarch contended, are to be faithful to their husbands. But for a husband, no such limitations apply. He commended the Persian kings who engaged in orgies for their restraint in waiting until they had sent their wives away from the sight of such debauchery. Plutarch then added as a general principle that "if therefore any private person, swayed by the unruly motions of his incontinency, happen at any time to make a trip with a kind she-friend or his wife's chambermaid, it becomes not the wife presently to lower and take pepper in the nose, but rather to believe that it was his respect to her which made him unwilling she should behold the follies of inebriety and foul intemperance."[29]

The Jewish Devaluation of Women

Paul's Gentile converts to the faith were heirs to Greek philosophy, with Aristotelian and Stoic disdain for women. His Jewish converts were heirs to the authority of the Old Testament, which offers quite a varied and often colorful collection of examples of womanhood. The stories within its pages depict a great diversity of personalities and powers among women, including the cooperative spirit of the harlot Rahab, the gentle seductiveness of the widow Ruth, and the sexual cleverness of

Judah's daughter-in-law Tamar, and also including the military aggressiveness of Deborah, the assassin's courage of Jael, and the homocidal seductiveness of Judith. Women in the Old Testament were not always the passive and timid souls often portrayed by Sunday school curricula!

An ideal wife is described in Proverbs 31 as one who not only tends to household chores but also buys real estate, manages a household staff, oversees production from a vineyard, and engages in a linen garment manufacturing enterprise on the side. She is homemaker, administrator, and entrepreneur, working both day and night with an industriousness that wins the admiration of her family (and allows her husband the privilege of sitting all day at the city gates as a community leader).

But despite the examples of capable and stong-willed women in the Old Testament, the rabbis of Judaism (for the most part) devalued women in their teachings. To be sure, a few rabbis argued in favor of sexual equality. "Whether Israelite or Gentile, man or woman, male or female slaves," wrote one, "according to their works the Holy Spirit dwells also upon him." Another offered a similar thought, while still associating wives and slaves: "Before God, all are equal: women and slaves, poor and rich." But many other teachings deprecate womanhood. "Girls are but an illusory treasure," sighed one rabbi; "Besides, they have to be watched continually." Another remarked, "A woman has more pleasure in one *kab* [measure] with lechery than in nine *kabs* with modesty."[30]

These statements reflect the judgment of one of the authors of the writings of the Apocrypha, Jesus ben Sirach, who, early in the second century before Christ, lamented that

> A daughter keeps her father secretly wakeful,
>   and worry over her robs him of sleep;
> when she is young, lest she do not marry,
>   or if married, lest she be hated;
> while a virgin, lest she be defiled
>   or become pregnant in her father's house;

or having a husband, lest she prove unfaithful,
    or, though married, lest she be barren.
Keep strict watch over a headstrong daughter,
    lest she make you a laughingstock to your enemies,
a byword in the city and notorious among the people,
    and put you to shame before the great multitude.
Do not look upon any one for beauty,
    and do not sit in the midst of women;
for from the garments comes the moth,
    and from a woman comes woman's wickedness.
Better is the wickedness of a man than a woman who
does good;
    and it is a woman who brings shame and disgrace.
(Sir. 42:9–14 RSV)[31]

Questions about women arose within the teachings of the rabbis that related to the story of Adam and Eve, to the laws of the Old Testament regarding husbands and wives, and to the more immediate concern of whether or not females should be educated.

First, let us consider the story of Adam and Eve. In the beginning Adam is portrayed as incomplete without Eve, needing a "help meet" or "helper." The Hebrew word here is *ezer*. Some biblical scholars translate this as "partner" rather than "helper," because the latter implies a subordinate role. The word *ezer* in itself does not connote an inferior status. In fact, when it is not referring to Eve, it appears seventeen times in the Old Testament, and each time it refers to God.[32]

Eve is depicted as falling for the promises of a smooth-talking serpent, and as a result she is cursed with pain in childbearing and with an altered relationship with her husband. From this time on, her husband will rule over her. Meanwhile, Adam (who has followed Eve's example in disobedience to God) is cursed with earning his bread with the sweat of his brow. The ground that Adam tills will now bear thistles and thorns. Such is the pitiable state of the first human family after the curse: the husband works long hours with little reward, and then he comes home and rules his wife, who desires her husband and who bears children with great painfulness (Gen. 3:16–19).

A great variety of interpretations have arisen from the wording of the first three chapters of Genesis, regarding the creation of Adam and Eve and their disobedience and fall. Some of these interpretations serve as mere curios from the history of religious thought. For example, some have believed that Adam was bisexual at first, and that since the separating of Eve from Adam's side, human beings have been incomplete, seeking a reunion through coitus. Some ancients taught that Adam attempted sexual intercourse with all the animals before he was given Eve as the perfect mate. Others interpreted the act of eating the fruit of the tree of knowledge of good and evil as a euphemism for copulation.

Other interpretations have centered upon the relationship of men and women inasmuch as Adam and Eve symbolize the whole human race. Some have argued that since Adam was made before Eve, Adam (male) is superior to Eve (female). It is interesting to note that no one has carried out this basis of ranking according to the order of creation to its logical conclusion: that cows are superior to man, since cows were created before Adam, and fish are superior to cows, since they were created first, and so on. The order in which the first couple fell to temptation has been given more attention, however, with the conclusion that since Eve sinned first, women are more easily led into error than are men. Moreover, since Adam was tempted by Eve, one must conclude that women constitute a moral threat to men.

Three other equally plausible interpretations seem to have been overlooked in the history of Jewish and Christian thought, omissions that in themselves are cause for reflection. The first interpretation focuses upon the fact that the serpent waited until Eve was alone before tempting her. This has been interpreted, traditionally, as demonstrating that women are morally more vulnerable and easily led astray than men. The account could just as well suggest that husbands and wives are meant to provide each other with moral fortitude, and when this fails, sin can enter into their relationship and change it.

The second interpretation suggests that the serpent deliberately chose Eve because she was the stronger, not the weaker, of the two. After all, it took all of the skill of the temptor to lead Eve to sin, while the simple act of handing the forbidden fruit to Adam was sufficient to lead him to sin. The serpent may have chosen the stronger of the two, knowing that if she fell for his line, the other would follow her example.

The third interpretation is the least speculative of the three. It focuses upon the result of sin for the couple, in which she desires him and he rules over her. If this kind of marital relationship, far from being divinely ordered, is the product of sin and God's curse, then it is to be avoided rather than commended. It is characteristic of marriage outside of God's grace. To prescribe that kind of relationship is to advocate living under the penalty of sin imposed upon Adam and Eve, as if Christ brought nothing new to marriage relationships.

Let us turn now to consider how one of the laws of the Old Testament affected the Jewish view of the relationship between husbands and wives. One of the Ten Commandments became the basis for the legal principle within Judaism that married women are the property of their husbands. Often this commandment, the tenth, is shortened to the phrase "Thou shalt not covet," but its full wording contains an implication that the doctors of the law did not overlook: "Neither shall you covet your neighbor's wife; and you shall not desire your neighbor's house, his field, or his manservant, or his maidservant, his ox, or his ass, or anything that is your neighbor's" (Deut. 5:21 RSV).[33]

Rabbinical interpretation reasoned that all the potential objects of a person's coveting, as listed in this commandment, are the possessions of that person's neighbor: his ass, his ox, his servants, his field, his house—and his wife. One can covet (Hebrew *chamad*) only that which belongs to another. Therefore, they argued, since coveting a man's wife is mentioned, then a man's wife must be his possession. The commandment, they added, makes no distinction between field, animal, servant, or wife.

Because of this interpretation, women were granted few legal rights of their own in ancient Israel. A husband could refuse even to acknowledge any business agreement entered into by his wife, and the injured party had no legal recourse (just as in our own country parents may refuse to acknowledge any business agreement entered into by their child, if she or he is a minor). An unmarried woman was regarded as the possession of her father, and a widow as the possession of her husband's male next-of-kin. She could inherit, but her inheritance would be put in trust for her, managed by the man who was in charge of her care.[34]

Now in one sense this notion of women being possessions was good in that they were guaranteed the necessities of life, as long as some man was alive who was given the responsibility of each woman's care. But it also meant that women were regarded as objects, not persons, alive but inferior to men. One illustration of this lower status was the practice of women's not eating with men. A wife would serve her husband at the table and stand while he ate.

Women, when regarded as objects, could be coveted or protected. But they could also be feared and avoided. Women who appeared in public in ancient Israel were enveloped in social mores that both protected them and isolated them. For example, it was regarded as improper for a man to speak to a woman in public, even if she were his own wife. And if she spoke to a man in the street, she was presumed to have a relationship with him that was improper; indeed, for this act her husband could divorce her without having to return her dowery.[35] She would be regarded as an adulteress.

This did not mean that a man might not converse with a friend's wife, however; but such an act was discouraged. A Rabbi Jahanan admonished, "Talk not much with womankind. They said this of a man's own wife; how much more of his fellow's wife! Hence the Sages have said: He that talks much with womankind brings evil upon himself and neglects the study of the Law and at last will inherit Gehenna."[36] (At a later date a woman named Beruriah ridiculed the rabbinical attitude toward women and this teaching in particular during an exchange between her and a certain Rabbi Jose from Galilee. While on a journey he met Beruriah and asked her, "By what road do we go to Lydda?" She responded, "Foolish Galilean! Did not the Sages say this: 'Engage not in much talk with women'? You should have asked: 'By which to Lydda?'"[37]) A rabbi might not speak even to his own daughter in public, or his own sister. And some of the Pharisees were referred to as "the bruised and bleeding ones" because they would shut their eyes whenever they saw a woman on the street, and therefore they often walked into walls and houses.[38]

This code of customs and prohibitions was not simply a curious means of demonstrating respect and honor to women. Behind it is the attitude within the prayer that every Jewish male was enjoined to recite each morning, thanking God that "He did not make me a Gentile, . . . a woman, . . . a boor."[39]

Finally, let us consider the question of educating women. This issue was never wholly settled within ancient Judaism. "It would be better to see the Torah [the laws of God in scripture] burnt than to hear its words upon the lips of women," insisted one rabbi. Another averred that "teaching a girl is the same as starting her on the road to depravity." Still another taught, "If any man gives his daughter a knowledge of the Law it is as though he taught her lechery." However, a more moderate voice insisted that "every man is required to teach his daughter the Torah."[40] If a girl were to receive an education, then, the duty fell upon her father rather than upon her mother or the synagogue school —that is, if her father were alive, if her father himself were educated, and if he agreed with the minority voice that affirmed the value of education for girls.

An Example of Cultural Bias Leading to
Misinterpretation of Scripture

The deprecation of womanhood within Judaism during this period of history was too extensive, one suspects, to depend solely upon any interpretation of Scripture as its source. The interpretations themselves regarding women seem so forced that one must assume these scholars first held a bias against women and then imposed that attitude upon the words of Scripture.

A case in point is the interpretation of the last of the Ten Commandments, prohibiting coveting. As mentioned previously, rabbinical scholars supposed that the wording in this commandment demonstrated that women are possessions of their husbands. In order to impose such an interpretation, however, one must rip this commandment out of its context and read it without regard for the other nine commandments.

One of the basic principles of biblical study is the necessity of considering the meaning of a portion of Scripture within its own context. Just as one may distort the intention of a speaker by quoting bits and snatches of his or her speech, so one may err in understanding Scripture by disregarding the words preceding and following a key passage. The misinterpretation of the tenth commandment that robs women of legal rights illustrates this danger.

The rabbinical interpretation is correct in noting that coveting is a wrong desire. It is a longing to take and own that which belongs to another. The Hebrew word for coveting, *chamad*, suggests a deep desire, a lusting after something. When the object of one's desire is owned by someone else, that attitude is wrong and is forbidden. *Chamad* can become an ugly, selfish longing within a person's heart that leads to a disregard for the rights and feelings of others.

Since the commandment against *chamad* specifically mentions another man's wife, the commandment seems to imply that wives are the property of their husbands—if one reads this commandment alone, isolated from the others. (Unfortunately, this same tendency to tear portions of Scripture out of context is sometimes used by persons who read Paul's writings in the fifth chapter of Ephesians, in which they find that wives are to be subject to their husbands, but overlook the preceding instruction that all Christians are to be subject to one another, and overlook the subsequent instruction that husbands are to love their wives as Christ loved the Church. See chapter 2.)

The subject matter of the tenth commandment is an attitude. It forbids coveting. It does not forbid stealing. The eighth commandment has already done that ("neither shall you steal"). It does not forbid adultery. The seventh commandment has already done that ("neither shall you commit adultery"). It forbids lusting after the possessions of another, whether or not this kind of desire leads to any sort of action. The tenth commandment is not about wives. It is about a wrong attitude, which may be directed toward the wife of another. Does this possibility mean that wives are among the possessions of their husbands? Are wives of the same status as slaves or houses, since all these may be the objects of covetousness?

The fifth commandment begins with the words "Honor your father and your mother." The wife of one's father is to receive honor. Now, things cannot receive honor. Possessions cannot receive honor. Only persons can receive honor, and this commandment gives equal value to a wife and mother as to a husband and father. (A person may admire the possession of another, but to honor it would be dangerously close to idolatry.) Wives are not things, according to the fifth commandment.

The seventh commandment forbids adultery, the sexual violation of a marriage contract. Faithfulness in marriage was taken very seriously in the law of Moses; both men and women who committed adultery were regarded as responsible and both were given the same punishment. (Lev. 20:10). Now, a marriage contract can be formed only between two persons who have the freedom to form such a contract. And adultery is a sexual violation of the marriage contract. But a slave had no sexual claims upon her (or his) master, and therefore a person could not commit adultery against a slave.[41]

Hence, the fifth and seventh commandments contravene the notion that wives are possessions of their husbands. A wife is not an object nor a slave, since one cannot honor a thing nor commit adultery against a slave.

How, then, can a man covet his neighbor's wife if she is not a possession? *He can do so only if he begins with the erroneous assumption that women are to be owned and used for man's own pleasure.* Coveting a neighbor's house is a wrong attitude about another's possession. Coveting his wife is a wrong attitude about his wife, based on another wrong attitude about women in general.

Therefore, the tenth commandment does not imply that wives are to be regarded as possessions along with slaves and oxen and asses and houses. Instead, it condemns the desire based on the attitude that regards wives as possessions along with slaves and oxen and asses and houses! By taking this commandment out of context, the interpreters forced it to defend the very attitude about women that it in fact forbids!

As we shall see, the same misuse has been made of many of Paul's writings about women. That which he opposed, his own words have been quoted to defend.

The Hellenization of Jewish Thought and Scripture

How could dedicated scholars of Hebrew Scripture make this kind of blunder in interpretation? Perhaps they began with a belief in the inferiority of women—a belief that had its source outside of Scripture—which they then imposed upon Scripture.

One such source was the Hellenization of Jewish thought after the conquest of Judea by Alexander the Great. Many of the Jews welcomed the customs and philosophy of the Greeks. They found them refreshing. The author of the apocryphal book I Maccabees described this Hellenizing process:

At that time, lawless men arose in Israel and seduced many with their plea, "Come, let us make a covenant with the gentiles around us, because ever since we have kept ourselves separated from them we have suffered many evils." The plea got so favorable a reception that some of the people took it upon themselves to apply to the king, who granted them liberty to follow the practices of the gentiles. Thereupon they built a gymnasium in Jerusalem according to the custom of the gentiles and underwent operations to disguise their circumcision, rebelling against the sacred covenant. They joined themselves to the gentiles and became willing slaves to evildoing. (1 Macc. 1:11–15 RSV)[42]

It is no accident that the writer focused upon the erection of a gymnasium in Jerusalem as a symbol of Hellenization. In Greek culture, the gymnasium was the center not only of physical education and recreation, but also of literary education in classical Greek philosophy. In the gymnasium, men engaged in exercise in the nude, which would have brought attention to the matter of circumcision (and which would have shocked the conservative Jews). And in the gymnasium young Jewish men learned the philosophical insights of Plato and Aristotle and the Stoics, which contained the doctrine of the inferiority of women.

The influence of Greek thought within Judaism was subtle and far-reaching. Even the prayer in which every Jewish man thanked God that He did not make him a Gentile, a woman, or a boor, had its origin not within Judaism, but within Greek thought, some scholars have argued.[43] Certainly Plutarch and others observed that Thales, Socrates, and Plato fostered the sentiments contained within this prayer.

Greek Stoic philosophy not only regarded women as inferior to men, but also as a danger to the man who would pursue wisdom and ascetic discipline. Like the Stoics, the Essenes, a radical movement within Judaism, also advocated an extreme form of ascetic discipline and regarded women as a hindrance to the man who would pursue holy wisdom.[44] (This same concern over the way a wife might inhibit her husband's study of Scripture and the law of God continued into the following centuries among rabbis. In the Talmud is expressed the opinion that some men may come down with croup as a punishment for neglecting their studies, and that some women may suffer from the same malady for restraining their husbands from their studies.⁴⁵)

Just as some Stoic philosophers were married, so were some of the Jewish Essenes. But the most notable group within that sect lived in a monastic community at Qumran, beside the Dead Sea, and produced the famous Dead Sea Scrolls. In these writings, the term *flesh* denotes human character at its basest, and female flesh symbolizes this most of all. Magen Broshi, in an article entitled "Beware the Wiles of the Wanton Woman," demonstrates how this literary symbolism denigrates female sexuality:

Certain metaphors recur frequently in the Dead Sea Scrolls, indicating Essene abhorence of sexuality. Sometimes the full impact is lost in translation. For example, in one translation of the Thanksgiving Scroll man is described as "a creature of clay, kneaded in water, a fundament of shame and a source of pollution" (i, 21–22). Actually, the word *ervah*, translated as "shame," is really "pudenda," and *nidah*, translated as "pollution," is really "menstration." These terms occur dozens of times in the scrolls.⁴⁶

The tendency toward the Hellenization of Jewish thought was given formal sanction in the writings of Philo, a Jewish scholar in Alexandria at the time of Christ. He sought to harmonize the teachings of Plato and Aristotle and other Greek philosophers with the teachings of the Old Testament. In the process, he imposed the Greek disdain for women onto his interpretation of Scripture (just as later Christian scholars were to do in their interpretations of the writings of Paul). True to Greek thought, Philo taught that

there is in the soul a male and female element just as there is in families, the male corresponding to the men, the female to the women. The male soul assigns itself to God alone as the Father and Maker of the Universe and the Cause of all things. The female clings to all that is born and perishes; it stretches out its faculties like a hand to catch blindly at what comes in its way, and gives the clasp of friendship to the world of created things with all its numberless changes and trans- mutations, instead of to the divine order, the immutable, the blessed, the thrice happy.[47]

Philo viewed the statement in Genesis 2 of how a man shall "cleave unto his wife" with disfavor. He interpreted it from the mindset of Aristotelian philosophy, which states that a husband is to his wife as one's soul is to one's body:

In us mind corresponds to man, the senses to woman; and pleasure encounters and holds parley with the senses first, and through them cheats with her quackeries the sovereign mind itself. . . . In a word we must never lose sight of the fact that Pleasure, being a courtesan and a wanton, eagerly desires to meet with a lover, and searches for panders, by whose means she shall get one on her hook. It is the senses that act as panders for her and procure the lover. When she has ensnared these she easily brings the Mind under her control.[48]

Therefore, man "leaves" his father (that is, Philo argued, a man leaves God) and becomes "one passion" with his wife.[49]

In practice, Philo would have females confined to the home.

Market-places and council-halls and law-courts and gatherings and meetings where a large number of people are assembled, and open- air life with full scope for discussion and action—all these are suitable to men both in war and in peace. The women are best suited to the indoor life which never strays from the house, within which the mid- dle door is taken by the maidens as their boundary, and the outer door by those who have reached full womanhood.[50]

But Philo defended the Essene ideal of celibacy, arguing along with the Stoics that "a wife is a selfish creature . . . adept at beguiling the morals of her husband."[51]

In the next generation after Philo, Josephus, a Jewish histo- rian who also studied both Greek and Hebrew literature, viewed the Old Testament with the same disdain toward wom- en. He wrote how the Jewish law declared that the wife "is inferior to her husband in all things."[52] He even went beyond the Jewish law in the matter of witnesses in a court of law, insisting that the testimony of women should not be admitted "on account of their levity and the boldness of their sex."[53]But not all Jewish scholars agreed with the Aristotelian view of womanhood nor welcomed the Greek attitude toward females. One notable exception was Gamaliel, the teacher of Saint Paul. He told a delightful story illustrating the worth of women. In it, an emperor expressed his own interpretation of the creation story. "Your God is a thief," the emperor said to a Jewish sage, "for in order to make the woman he had to steal a rib from the sleeping Adam."

The wise man, Gamaliel went on to say, did not know how to reply to this criticism of God. But the wise man's daughter, hearing what had been said, went to the emperor and cried, "We demand justice!"

"What for?" asked the ruler.

"Thieves broke into our house in the night. They took away a silver ewer," she explained, "and they left a gold one in its place."

The emperor laughed and replied, "I wish I could have burglars like that every night!"

"Well," said the woman, "that is what our God did. He took a mere rib from the first man and in exchange for it he gave him a wife."[54]

The attitude reflected in this tale was part of the educational heritage of the apostle Paul, who later wrote in defiance of those who would deprecate women that there is "neither male nor female, for you are all one in Christ Jesus."

Seeing Paul Through the Eyes of Aristotle

Unfortunately, the Gentiles whom Paul sought to convert to a faith in Jesus Christ brought with them the Greek notions of female inferiority, espoused the same interpretations of the Old Testament as those of the Hellenized Jews, and used Paul's writings to give authority to the same philosophical viewpoint that Paul opposed.

For example, Tertullian (c. A.D. 160–230), a leading defender of the Christian faith, used the traditional interpretation of Eve's sin to condemn all women. He wrote, "woman . . . do you not know that you are (each) an Eve? The sentence of God on this sex of yours lives in this age: the guilt must of necessity live too. *You* are the devil's gateway: *you* are the unsealer of that (forbidden) tree: *you* are the first deserter of the divine law: *you* are she who persuaded him whom the devil was not valiant enough to attack. *You* destroyed so easily God's image in man. On account of *your* desert—that is, death—even the Son of God had to die."[55]

Tertullian was a Roman lawyer, schooled in Stoic philosophy. His attitude toward women reflects that Greek heritage.

Saint Augustine, who, like Tertullian, had been schooled in Stoic philosophy, regarded marriage as "a covenant with death."[56] Both he and Saint Jerome (who translated the Bible into Latin, a version that became the standard translation for the Roman Catholic church) regarded celibacy as a more holy state than marriage for Christians.

The moral laxity of Roman society led many conscientious Christians to adandon all worldly wealth and pleasures and to flee into the ascetic disciplines of desert hermitages and monasteries. In the spirit of the Jewish Essenes and Greek Stoics, they also abandoned the option of marriage in their pursuit of personal holiness. The celibacy of these devout desert fathers was admired by those who espoused Greek philosophy. For example, Galen, a Greek physician in Rome during the latter part of the second century after Christ, observed that

as a rule, men need to be educated in parables. Just as in our day we see those who are called Christians have gained their faith from parables. Yet they sometimes act exactly as true philosophers would. That they despise death is a fact we all have before our eyes; and by some impulse of modesty they abstain from sexual intercourse—some among them, men and women, have done so all their lives. And some, in ruling and controlling themselves, and in their keen passion for virtue, have gone so far that real philosophers could not excel them.[57]

It would be natural for a Christian monk, regarding sexual desire as a hindrance to meditation, to go a step further and view sexual desires as evil. From that point, it is but another small step to view the objects of sexual desire—women—as snares in the narrow pathway to purity, and to conclude (along with the Essenes) that women are symbolic of the basest of human corruption.

Clement, a liberal theologian in Alexandria later in the second century after Christ, objected to those Christians who held up Jesus' example of celibacy and regarded marriage as simple prostitution and a practice introduced by the devil.[58]

This tendency to interpret Scripture from the viewpoint of Greek philosophy was finally given highest expression in the thirteenth century in the writings of Thomas Aquinas (c. 1225–1274), whose gentle spirit and brilliant mind inspired those who knew him to refer to him as the Angelic Doctor. Aquinas did more than any other to systematize Christian beliefs and to harmonize them with Greek philosophy (see chapter 7). In this monumental task, Aquinas interpreted the writings of Saint Paul through the mind of Aristotle, and the Greek deprecation of women became solidly infused within Christian theology.

Since that time, both Catholics and Protestants have tended to read Paul's words through the eyes of pagan philosophers who lived five centuries before the apostle!

Questions for Thought and Discussion

1. If the people of Athens had followed Socrates' suggestion of having women educated and performing the same tasks as men, what difference do you think this would have made in subsequent history?
2. Aristotle assumed that a leader among bees must be male, since leadership (he believed) is a masculine quality. Can

you think of other examples in nature, besides that of bees, in which females take leadership roles?

3. Married women in Athens were restricted to home and the care of children. What were the advantages of this kind of lifestyle? The disadvantages?

4. The Jewish Essenes regarded all Gentiles with disdain, and yet their ideas about women and marriage were very similar to those of the Greek philosophers. Is it possible that they were influenced by Greek thought? Do people sometimes believe what they hear their enemies teaching?

5. If women were regarded as the legal responsibility of their fathers or husbands in our society today, what changes would this make?

6. What are the advantages of the custom of arranged marriages (in which one's mate is chosen by one's parents)? The disadvantages? Which do you prefer?

7. If Adam had fallen to temptation before Eve did, would this change the way some people regard women?

2. New Roles for Husbands and Wives

A few years after Paul was executed in Rome, a volcano in southern Italy called Vesuvius erupted and buried in its ash the city of Pompeii.

Excavations have recovered from that wealthy Roman seaport a vast assortment of artworks centering on themes of mythology, male sex organs, and erotic pleasures. One mosaic, however, is different. It captures the drama of a historic event, the battle of Issus (333 B.C.), in which Alexander the Great defeated Darius III of Persia. In this masterfully crafted scene (which, incidentally, was a copy of a fourth-century B.C. Greek painting), young Alexander is depicted as one whose entire energy and intellect is focused upon the task at hand, extending his control and creating a vast empire across the Mediterranean, into Africa, and as far east as India.

Three centuries later another young man sought to weld together the same lands that Alexander and his army of Hellenes had conquered—but this individual was without any army. Armed only with a faith and the news of an executed Jew who was raised from the dead, Paul envisioned a world in which Jews and Greeks, educated and barbarian, slaves and free, men and women would be equal citizens in a kingdom that was not political but spiritual. The lands that Alexander had Hellenized the apostle now wanted to Christianize. And in order to do that, Paul had to tear down the walls that Greek culture and philosophy had solidified between people—including walls between men and women, husbands and wives.

In order to establish this new way of faith in Christ, Paul had to interpret Christ's teachings and then to persuade his converts to transform their way of thinking and interacting to conform to these teachings.

Just as the relationship of Jewish husbands and wives tended to reflect the condition of Adam and Eve after the fall ("your husband shall rule over you"), so the relationship of Gentile husbands and wives tended to reflect the philosophy of Aristotle ("the courage of a man is shown in commanding, of a woman in obeying"). In Paul's gospel, a new order was at hand, in which all persons "are one in Christ Jesus." Now the relationship of Christian husbands and wives was to reflect the new model provided by the relationship of Christ and his church.

At first glance, the notion of patterning a marriage relationship after that of Christ and the Church may seem static, ethereal, and impractical. By medieval times, artists pictured Christ as passively looking at some distant mystical reality while gently lifting his right hand with three fingers extended; and they pictured the Church as a woman kneeling at the feet of Christ, head turned up to gaze at his halo with adoring eyes, wavy locks cascading down her back. No imagery could be more remote from Paul's radical teaching of the way Christ's relationship with his church serves as a model for Christian marriages.

And yet how this model has been misunderstood!

"The Ephesians 5 Syndrome"

At a workshop on marriage and family counseling, the noted author and pastoral counselor Howard Clinebell, Jr., made reference to how some people defend the patriarchal model of marriage (in which the husband has God-given authority over his wife) on the basis of Paul's teachings. Clinebell added that he has nicknamed this "the Ephesians 5 syndrome."

He was alluding to Paul's words in his letter to the church at Ephesus, specifically chapter 5, verses 21 through 33, in which the apostle appeals to couples in that congregation to follow his radical new model for Christian marriage. That portion of

Scripture has been cited time and again by those who would defend the concept of male superiority over females. However, the subject of the writing is not men and women, generally, but only husbands and wives (and, more specifically, Christian husbands and wives, since the model presupposes a faith in Christ). Moreover, a close study of Paul's words in Ephesians 5 reveals that he was writing against the concept of male superiority rather than defending it!

Paul wrote in a dialect of the Greek language called *koine* (pronounced coy-in-AY). Years ago, some Bible scholars supposed that *koine* Greek was invented in heaven and used only in the writings of the New Testament—a sort of holy language. But in fact *koine* was the most widely spoken and written language of Paul's time, understood by more people across the ancient world than any other. Latin was the tongue of the Roman conquerors, but its use was limited to a relatively small percentage of people.

Many thousands of scraps of everyday writings in *koine* Greek have been recovered in recent years, such as legal contracts, bills of sale, personal letters, and so forth. When the apostle Paul wrote to churches and individuals, he did so in this language, the one that could be read by almost any literate person and, when read out loud, could be understood by the greatest number of listeners. It was the language common to all those nations that had been subjected by Alexander the Great.

But modern translations of the New Testament cannot give us a complete and faithful rendering of what Paul wrote, simply because the meanings of words and phrases in any language can never be fully embodied in a translation into another language. And sometimes this difficulty in translating can lead to extremely serious misunderstandings. For example, when Nikita Kruschev told the American people, "We will bury you," the words chilled the hearts of his listeners and dramatically escalated the cold war and the sale of plans for building bomb shelters. But the actual Russian words spoken by Kruschev, as one translator pointed out to anyone still listening, did not contain a threat of war. The English translation implied that the Soviets were going to kill the population of the United States. However, the actual words only meant something like "by the time this present generation has passed on, the political system of the United States will be communism." The literal translation implied a threat to kill, but the meaning of the original words in Russian only offered a prediction (however dire and unrealistic it might be!).

In the same way, Paul's words about husbands and wives may be misunderstood when translated word for word into another language. Therefore, one must examine what Paul actually wrote, rather than just a translation.

Unfortunately, the Greek language has a reputation for being complex and inscrutable, as the phrase "it's all Greek to me" suggests. But such, happily, is not the case. Those who do not have a working knowledge of *koine* Greek can nonetheless learn the meanings of a few key words and phrases used by Paul and thereby discover the original meaning of Paul's radical model for marriage. (From this point on, *koine* Greek will be referred to simply as Greek, for the sake of simplicity.)

A translation of Eph. 5:21–33, in this case not from any specific version but typifying several modern translations, reads like this:

Be subject to one another in reverence for Christ. Wives, be subject to your husbands as to the Lord. For the husband is head of the wife, as Christ is head of the church, his body, and is himself savior of the body. But as the church is subject to Christ, so also let the wives be subject to their husbands in everything. Husbands, love your wives, as Christ loved the church and gave himself up for her, that he might sanctify her, having cleansed her by the washing of water with the word, that he might present the church to himself in all glory, without spot or wrinkle or any such thing, that she should be holy and unblemished. So husbands ought also to love their wives as their own bodies. He who loves his wife loves himself. For no man ever hated his own flesh, but nourishes and cherishes it, as Christ does the church, because we are members of his body. "For this reason a man shall leave his father and mother and be joined to his wife, and the two shall become one." This mystery is great, but I say it in reference to Christ and the church. However, let each and every one of you love his wife as himself, and let the wife see that she respects her husband.

Even in the English translation, one may note that the scope of this passage is limited to husbands and wives (except the first sentence, which is directed to all members of the Church). Moreover, although this scripture is often lifted up in reference to women, more of it is written to husbands than to wives (in the Greek, 47 words are directed at wives while 143 are directed at husbands).

Now, there are three key words in this passage that embody the concepts within the new model Paul presented for Christian couples, words that are easily misunderstood when translated into English.

Key Word #1: *Head*

"The husband is head of the wife," Paul explained, "as Christ is head of the church." In English, the word *head* means literally the physical head of one's body and figuratively the leader of a body of people. The two meanings are intertwined.

Not so in Greek, where two different and distinct words are translated "head." One of these is *arche* (pronounced ar-KAY). It means "head" in terms of leadership and point of origin. It was used to denote "beginning" in the sense of the first or point of inception (and we use this Greek word as a prefix in such words as *archaeology*, *archetype*, and *archives*, all relating to old or first things). Just as it was used to denote point of origin, so we use *head* that way in the word *headwaters* (of a river). *Arche* was also used to denote "first" in terms of importance and power (and we use it as a prefix in such words as *archangel*, *archbishop*, *archenemy*, *archduke*, and so on, all relating to the head of a group in terms of leadership). Forms of *arche* are used throughout the New Testament, including the writings of Paul, to designate the head or leader of a group of people. These forms are translated "magistrate," "chief," "prince," "ruler," "head," and so forth.

Now, in the Bible we find many puns, not as a form of humor so much as a form of wisdom, where a word was used that meant two things, both of which were true and were intended to be understood by the one word. For example, Jesus told a woman in Samaria that he would give her "living" water (John 7:10), and the word translated "living" also means "running." Another time Jesus "breathed" on his disciples and told them to "receive Holy Spirit" (John 20:22); in Greek (and also in Hebrew) the word for "spirit" also means "breath."

Therefore, if Paul had believed as Aristotle taught, that husbands should command their wives and rule over them, then Paul could have made a pun out of the word *arche*. He could have written that the husband is the *arche* (head) of the wife, and in that one sentence he would have meant that the husband is to rule over the wife and at the same time have reminded his readers how man (Adam) was the source of woman (Eve, who was formed of Adam's rib). Both senses of *arche* (ruler, and point of origin) would have been invoked.[1]

However, Paul did not chose to use the word *arche* when he wrote of how the husband is head of his wife. He was well aware of that word, but he deliberately chose a different term.

Instead, Paul used the word *kephale* (pronounced kef-ah-LAY). This word does mean "head," the part of one's body. It was also used to mean "foremost" in terms of position (as a capstone over a door, or a cornerstone in a foundation). It was never used to mean "leader" or "boss" or "chief" or "ruler." *Kephale* is also a military term. It means "one who leads," but not in the sense of "director." *Kephale* did not denote "general," or "captain," or someone who orders the troops from a safe distance; quite the opposite, a *kephale* was one who went before the troops, the leader in the sense of being in the lead, the first one into battle.

Therefore, two words in Greek can both be translated into the one English word *head*. One word means "boss," the other means "physical head" (or, sometimes, "the first soldier into battle"). Unfortunately, an English-speaking person who reads that the husband is head of his wife will normally conclude that this means the husband is to rule over his wife. This is what Aristotle taught and what most Hellenized people thought. The husband is an *arche* to his wife, head of the household and ruler over all his family. Paul deliberately chose the other word. But people who depend on the English translation cannot know that.

Can one be certain that *arche* and *kephale* were so different from each other in meaning? Could *kephale* not sometimes mean "boss" or "ruler"? One way to be certain is to note how these two words were used in the Septuagint. The Old Testament, except for a few portions, was written in Hebrew. But by the age of Paul, few persons could read that language. Instead, they depended upon a translation of the Old Testament from Hebrew into Greek, which was called the Septuagint. Paul was familiar with this translation and quoted from it.

Now, in Hebrew, just as in English, one word means both "physical head" and "ruler." The word is *rosh*. If *arche* and *kephale* were more or less synonymous and could be used interchangeably, then when the seventy scholars who wrote the Septuagint came to the Hebrew word *rosh*, they could have used either Greek word as they wished, or instead just used one of the two all the time. However, they were very careful to note how the word *rosh* was used, whether it meant "physical head" or "ruler of a group." Whenever *rosh* meant "physical head," they translated it *kephale*; or whenever *rosh* referred to the first soldier leading others into battle with him, they also translated it *kephale*. But when *rosh* meant "chief" or "ruler," they translated it *arche* or some form of that word.[2] Every time, this distinction was carefully preserved.

Paul was certainly familiar with both words. He knew the language, he read and quoted from the Septuagint, and he used both words in his own writing. The difference between the two would have been obvious to him. Modern readers, however, may misunderstand Paul, assuming that the word for head that Paul used also carried the figurative meaning of "boss" or "ruler." Paul in fact took great care not to say that.

Key Word #2: *Be Subject To*

In the translation of Eph. 5:21–33 given earlier, the words *be subject to* appear three times. Church members are to be subject to one another, and wives are to be subject to their husbands just as the Church is subject to Christ. Three kinds of relationships are defined by a key word that is usually translated "be subject to."

This phrase in English may bring to mind images from children's fairy tales of medieval settings, with kings and their subjects. "Be subject to" may sound like a command to bow before the ruler, who sits on his throne dressed in ermine and holding a jeweled gold scepter. And one might then assume that Paul was telling wives that they are to obey their husbands as a subject would obey the king.

Now, if the word translated "head" meant "boss," then husbands are to rule their wives; and the word translated "be subject to" would naturally mean "to obey." But since *kephale* does not mean "ruler" or convey any sense of leadership (aside from meaning "the first into battle"), then perhaps the word Paul used that is translated "be subject to " does not convey a sense of obedience. In fact, the use of that word in verse 21 ("be subject to one another") clearly demonstrates that it does not mean obedience, for it would be as impossible for a group of people to be obedient to each other as it would be for a group to follow each other.

Now, in Greek there is a word that means "to obey." It can be translated "be subject to," but it carries the idea of dutiful obedience. It is *hupakouo* (pronounced hoop-ah-KOO-o), a word that a master might use regarding a slave. And Paul knew this word. In fact, he used it a few sentences later in reference to slaves (Eph. 6:5). But while Greek philosophers would place both wives and slaves under the authority of men, Paul had no thought of wives being like slaves to their husbands, so he did not use this word. It is not the word that is translated "be subject to."

Moreover, in Greek there is another word that means "be subject to" and "obey." It is *peitharcheo* (peith-ar-KAY-o), one of the words built upon *arche*, "ruler." This is a word that a parent might use concerning a child. Paul knew this word, too. In fact, he used it a few sentences later in reference to children (Eph. 6:1). But while Greek philosophers would place wives under the tutelage of their husbands, and while the custodianship of a Jewish girl was passed at the time of her marriage directly from her father to her husband, Paul had no thought of wives being like children to their husbands, so he did not use this word. It is not the word that is translated "be subject to."

When referring to wives, Paul used a form of yet a different Greek word, *hupotasso* (hoop-o-TASS-o). It is not a word one would normally use regarding children or slaves. In its active form, *hupotasso* might be used of a conqueror concerning the vanquished. It means "to subject to," "to subordinate." But Paul did not use *hupotasso* in its active form to describe any person. He used it only to tell what God does. He did not tell husbands to *hupotasso* their wives.

Instead, Paul used this word in addressing wives only in its imperative, middle voice form (compare Col. 3:18). By writing it in the imperative mood, he was instructing wives. He was not describing them (as Aristotle did when he claimed that "the male is by nature fitter to command than the female"). Instead of describing them, he was appealing to them. And in writing the word in the middle voice form, he was emphasizing the voluntary nature of being "subject to."

This latter point needs an explanation. In English, verbs can be in the active or passive voice. In the active voice, the subject of the verb is acting. In the passive voice, the subject of the verb is being acted upon. Greek has the same active and passive voices. But it has also a third, middle voice, in which the subject of the verb is acting in a way that affects the subject.

It is difficult for English-speaking persons to grasp the subtle yet important distinction between middle and passive voice in Greek verbs just by reading the definition, and yet we think in ways that the Greek verb forms express. For example, a person may teach—an active verb. And, one may be taught—a passive verb. But a person may also teach himself or herself by careful listening, discovering, reasoning, learning. In that sense, the person is both subject and object of the action. That is what the Greek middle voice expresses, a voluntary action by the subject of the verb upon the subject of the verb.

Now, it would be possible in Greek to tell a person to subject someone else (although Paul never did so); and it would be possible to describe someone as being subject to another. But one cannot tell another to be subjected, any more than one can tell someone to be learned. However, Paul used *hupotasso* in the middle voice. This way, he was requesting that wives voluntarily, willingly, actively be subject to their husbands. This is the form *hupotassomai* (hoop-o-TASS-o-my). Since it is asking for something that is voluntary in nature, "be subject to" is an awkward translation at best. *Hupotassomai* means something like "give allegiance to," "tend to the needs of," "be supportive of," or "be responsive to." Perhaps the best meaning of *hupotassomai* is found in a German translation of that word, *sich unterstellen*, "to place oneself at the disposition of."[3]

There is, in addition, another meaning to *hupotassomai*. It also served as a military term, referring to taking a position in a phalanx of soldiers. In this sense, there is no reference to any idea of rank or status—it was an equal sharing of the task for which the soldiers were ordered. If a soldier failed to join the others, or held back during an advance, a captain might use a form of the verb *hupotassomai* to order him to return to the line, join his fellows, be supportive of them, fulfill his part of the assignment.

In that sense, Paul could tell all the members of the Church to be subject to (*hupotassomai*) one another, and he could also tell wives to be subject to their husbands. For *hupotassomai* is not a ranking of persons as ruler and ruled. It is a concise appeal for the Church to have its members live out their call to be "the body of Christ and individually members of it" (1 Cor. 12:27; compare Rom. 12:15; 1 Cor. 10:16–17; Eph. 2:16, 3:6, 4:4,16; Col. 1:18), to be willing to "bear one another's burdens, and so fulfill the law of Christ" (Gal. 6:2). What is true of the Church, Paul added, is to be true of a marriage.

Key Word #3: *Love*

Three times in the short passage in Ephesians about husbands and wives, Paul instructed husbands to love their wives, as if he needed to press the matter. The English word *love* has a scattered meaning, connoting everything from enjoyment of something to sexual intercourse. Therefore, translating Paul's appeal to read "Husbands, love your wives" leaves his meaning rather vague.

In Greek, there are several words for love. One of them is *erao* (er-AH-o), which denotes having sexual desire and passion. Paul did not command this kind of love—indeed, it is not something that can be commanded. There is also the word *phileo* (fill-EH-o), which means feeling fondness, friendship, a deep liking. It too is an emotional kind of love, a warmth that cannot be ordered into being. A third word is *agapao* (ah-ga-PAH-o), which has been popularized in recent years in its noun form, *agape* (ah-GA-pay). This kind of love is not so much a matter of emotion as attitude and action. It is the most frequently used form in the New Testament, and because it focuses upon a person's attitudes and actions, one can be asked to *agapao* someone. The great commandments use this word, telling us to love God and to love our neighbor. Jesus used this word in his instruction that we love our enemies. And Jesus defined this word in his parable of the good Samaritan, when a man helped another who was a stranger, an enemy, a victim who could not (and probably would not) repay the kindness.

Agapao is almost identical with *hupotassomai*. Both involve giving up one's self-interest to serve and care for another's. Both mean being responsive to the needs of the other. And both are commended to all Christians, as well as to husbands and wives.

In Jewish literature, a favorite form of writing involved using synonyms in parallel fashion. The Psalms illustrate this device repeatedly:

> Blessed is he whose transgression is forgiven,
> whose sin is covered. (Ps. 32:1 RSV)
> The earth is the Lord's and the fulness thereof,
> the world and those who dwell therein. . . . (Ps. 24:1 RSV)

In the section of Paul's letter to the Ephesians that we are considering, the apostle used two key words in just such a parallel fashion. Wives are to *hupotassomai* their husbands; husbands are to *agapao* their wives.

A New Model for Marriage: Christ's Relationship with His Church

Paul lifted up the relationship of Christ and the Church as a new model for Christian marriage. Christ is the head (*kephale*) of the Church, which is his body. Christ became head of the Church by giving himself up for the Church, even at the point of suffering death for his loved ones. Now, Christ is not head of the Church in order to rule the Church. He is not *arche* of the Church in that sense. One is reminded of Jesus' own perspective on being the kind of head that is boss versus the kind of head Paul had in mind: "And Jesus called them to him and said to them, 'You know those who are supposed to rule [Greek *archein*, the verb form of *arche*] over the Gentiles lord it over them, and their great men exercise authority over them. But it shall not be so among you; but whoever wishes to become great among you must be your servant, and whoever wishes to be first among you must be slave of all, for even the Son of man came not to be served but to serve, and to give his life as a ransom for many'"(Mark 10:42–45). Christ's aim was not to boss the Church, but to purify and sanctify it. In this sense, husbands are to be head of their wives, not to lord it over them, but to love them and serve them, just as wives are to be supportive of and serve their husbands.

Moreover, Paul would have husbands and wives be one with each other. He quoted Gen. 2:24, about how husband and wife "are to become one," just as the Church is to be one with Christ. Aristotle described a husband as the soul and his wife as the body; therefore, he argued, a husband is to rule his wife and a wife to obey her husband. Paul described a husband as the head of his wife as Christ is head of his church; therefore, a husband is to nourish and sanctify his wife and even be willing to die for her, and a wife is to be supportive of and responsive to the needs of her husband. More than a century after Paul, a Jewish sage expressed much the same thought when he said, "He who loves his wife as himself and honors her more than himself will guide his children along the right path."[4]

But centuries after that, the Christian theologian Thomas Aquinas assumed that Paul's analogy meant the same as Aristotle's. Based on that assumption, Aquinas wrote, "The relation of a husband to his wife is, in a certain way, like that of a master to his servant, insofar as the latter ought to be governed by the commands of his master." This great scholar missed the point of Paul's analogy, how being the head as Christ is the head of the Church means being a servant of all, being willing to give up life itself for the body. He overlooked Paul's admonition that the wife be responsive to the needs of (*hupotassomai*) her husband, and that the husband be responsive to the needs of (*aga-pao*) his wife. He missed the point when Paul lifted up the relationship of Adam and Eve before the fall, how they were one, and when Paul then commended that kind of unity to husbands and wives, through Christ. Aquinas was not aware of the subtle additional analogy of Paul's words in their military usage, implying that the husband is head when he sticks his neck out and goes first into battle, and that the wife is subject to her husband only by standing in formation with him, sharing the risks with him and obeying the same orders as he.

Unfortunately, those who must rely upon an English translation of Paul's writings will be subject to the same misinterpretations as those of Aquinas. There are simply no adequate terms in our language, no words that serve as exact equivalents to the three key words in Ephesians 5. Therefore, translating this passage is a very difficult task.

Key word #1, *kephale*, cannot be translated simply as "head" without suggesting a position of authority over those who are under the head, whereas *kephale* describes a position of risk, out in front, serving those who follow the head. How then can one better translate Paul's words "The husband is (head) of the wife"? Since *kephale* was a term used by the military, one might look for a suitable word within modern military terminology. Two such terms come to mind.

The first is *point*. It was borrowed from the cowboy language of the old West, when an individual would "ride point" and scout out the territory ahead. In the Vietnam War, an individual soldier would serve as the point by scouting ahead for traps, snipers, and bunkers. We might translate *kephale* as "point," but since that term is not well known in popular speech, readers would (excuse the pun) miss the point. Moreover, Paul himself used *kephale* as a pun, contrasting Christ as head with his church as body, and then extending this pun to the care and concern a man has for his body, commending a similar attitude within a man for his wife.

The second modern military term is *spearhead*. During World War II, the first soldiers sent into a new area or theater to engage the enemy in battle were called the spearhead. The spearhead would receive support from units behind them, of course, just as Paul tells wives to be supportive of their husbands; but translating Paul's words to read "the husband is the spearhead of the wife" would lead readers to all sorts of questionable conclusions!

Perhaps the only way to translate *kephale* is by paraphrasing Paul's words in such a manner as to remove the idea of "head" meaning "authority." The English would then convey the meaning of Paul's words rather than just the words themselves.

In the same way, key word #2, *hupotassomai*, cannot be translated simply "be subject to" without implying a subservient position. The phrase "be responsive to the needs of" expresses the essential meaning, but it is too long and unwieldy for a translation. "Serve" suggests the role of servant to master, and "minister to" might imply some unspecified but inherent weakness among husbands. Perhaps the phrase "be supportive of" is the most suitable among the choices offered by our language for a readable translation.

Key word #3, *agapao*, can also be translated "be responsive to the needs of," as long as that phrase does not imply weakness on the part of the recipient or grudging charity on the part of the benefactor. After all, Jesus used this same word in his commandment that we love God.

With special attention to these three key words, then, Paul's advice in Eph. 5:21–33 might be translated this way:

Be supportive of one another. Wives, be supportive of your husbands, as of the Lord. For the husband is head of the wife—that is, going ahead of her—in the same way as Christ is head of the church by being Savior of the body. But as the church is supportive of Christ, so let wives also be supportive of their husbands in everything. Husbands, be responsive to the needs of your wives as Christ has been to the church and gave himself up for her, in order that he might make her holy, cleansing her by the washing of water with the word, that he might present the church to himself in all glory, without spot or wrinkle or any such thing, that she should be holy and unblemished. So husbands ought also to respond to the needs of their wives as to their own bodies. He who responds to the needs of his own wife is responding to his own needs. For no man ever hated his own flesh, but nourishes and cherishes it, as Christ does the church, because we are members of his body. "For this reason a man shall leave his father and mother and be joined to his wife, and the two shall become one." This mystery is great, but I say it in reference to Christ and the church. However, let each and every one of you respond to the needs of his wife as to his own needs, and let the wife see that she respects her husband.

In a culture where husbands had little regard for the feelings and needs of their wives and where wives had little knowledge of the concerns of their husbands, Paul's advice to husbands and wives must have shocked his hearers! Small wonder that his instructions in empathy and supportiveness were soon interpreted to mean nothing more than a restatement of Aristotle's master/slave relationship. Jesus could say that "the Son of man came not to be served but to serve"; nonetheless, in the home the saying of the Greek philosopher prevailed: "The courage of a man is shown in commanding, of a woman in obeying."

In recent years considerable attention has been devoted to the task of shifting the basis of marriage in our society from romantic and sexual attraction to the kind of love that grows out of friendship. Marriages are more satisfying, advocates of this new model aver, if husbands and wives are friends who happen to have fallen in love with each other, experiencing the kind of love that is an extension of friendship. In other words, the best person for me to marry is one whom I like as well as love.

While Paul's words about husbands and wives are difficult to translate, they do present a radical new model for marriage that in many ways affirms this modern concept, yet goes beyond it as well. Husbands and wives were meant to be one from the very beginning, Paul pointed out. But this oneness, he declared, is to be like that of Christ and his church, expressed in loving and self-giving service to the other. This oneness is also to be like that between oneself and one's body. Sexual intimacy within marriage is a gift from God, and couples are not to refrain from such intimacy except when they mutually agree to do so, and then only for a brief time and for a specific purpose.

This model does leave many unexplored questions, however (such as the role of faith, hope, and grace within marriage, qualities that are so essential within the relationship of Christ and his church). But one conclusion is inescapable: Paul's model places the highest possible value upon marriage. Paul could pay no greater honor to the institution of marriage than he did, patterning marriage after the bond between the Savior and those whom he loved more than life itself.

Questions for Thought and Discussion

1. Can you think of ways the word head is used in our language to describe a person's role without implying that this person is a boss or ruler?

2. In what ways is Christ *arche* (ruler) of his church? In what ways is he *kephale* (head, as in pioneer or first into battle) of his church?

3. When is a husband most like a *kephale* to his wife?

4. *Hupotassomai* (be subject to) and *agapao* (love) are almost synonymous in that both require being responsive to the needs of another person. Consider the role of Greek and Jewish wives in Paul's day, and the role of their husbands. Why do you suppose that Paul used *hupotassomai* when addressing wives, and *agapao* when addressing husbands? Why does he use both words in saying how all Christians are to relate to one another?

5. Aristotle said that a husband is as soul to his wife, who is body. He used this analogy to support his conviction that

husbands should rule over their wives. In what ways does Paul's idea of a husband being head of his wife differ?

6. In what ways can a marriage relationship emulate the qualities of that between Christ and his church—faith, grace, hope, service?

3. Women as Leaders in the Church

The ancient synagogue at Capernaum, beside the north shore of the Sea of Galilee, remains one of the most memorable ruins in the Holy Land. The richness and beauty of its marble carvings impress the hundreds of visitors who enter it each day. A casual observer admires the lofty columns and assumes that these once supported a ceiling above the worshipers. And the same observer notices that the north wall seems to be intact and complete. However, if one moves behind the columns and gains an unobstructed view of that wall and from that position studies the line where the top edge of the wall meets the sky, he or she is surprised to find that this line is broken by an opening near the west end of the wall, like a large, solitary crenel in some medieval battlement. Closer examination reveals that this opening is simply the lower portion of a doorway. Suddenly one realizes that this wall, as it remains today, is missing a portion—a whole story—of its original height. And the columns, which at first glance appear to have supported the roof of the synagogue, are now seen as supports for what was once a balcony, accessible from the outside by some long-lost stairway that led to that mysterious doorway at the top of the wall.

Why was this balcony built above a portion of the main meeting room of the synagogue, and constructed in such a way that anyone seated there would be hidden from view and anyone entering or leaving would be forced to use steep outside stairs? The answer is that this was the place reserved for girls and women, just as the court of the women separated females from males outside the temple in Jerusalem. The front doors of the synagogue and the main floor—the meeting hall itself—were used exclusively by men. Women might be present in public worship, but only in a separate chamber, silent and unseen.

However restrictive such an arrangement might seem to us today, the Jewish custom of having women present at all during worship was innovative among ancient cultures in general (with the notable exception of Egypt). For the most part, when women did gather for worship it was usually in all-female company. For example, in Rome on a certain date in December the women of the city—or at least the women of higher social class—would meet in the home of one of the magistrates and worship the Bona Dea, the Good Goddess, led in worship by the Vestal Virgins. As with the mystery religions, the sacred rites were kept secret, although we know that these rites included the unveiling of sacred objects that could be shown only to women participants. Even the name of this goddess was not revealed to outsiders. The Bona Dea was most probably an earth deity who, it was believed, would promote women's fertility.

In the year 62 B.C., the worship of Bona Dea erupted in scandal. The meeting place was the home of Julius Caesar, at the invitation of his wife, Popeia. A certain young patrician named Publius Clodius, who was carrying on a love affair with Popeia according to reports, decided to disguise himself as a woman and, carrying a lute, enter with the participants. His deep voice gave him away, however, and the rituals were brought to a sudden end. Clodius was arrested and tried for the crime of sacrilege, while Popeia was divorced by Caesar.

Many of the public feasts and sacrifices of the worship of the old gods in Rome excluded women and slaves, or else included some women in a very specific and limited role. The inclusion of women in the Jewish synagogue worship (as hearers, at least) at the time of the inception of Christianity compares favorably with pagan worship.

One of the most important reasons behind the separation of the sexes during worship in ancient societies was the association of women in worship with cultic prostitution. As difficult as this may be for modern people to understand, sexual intercourse has been an integral part of worship within various past cultures of the Mediterranean world. Thus in the time of Paul the inclusion of women with men in worship would have regarded with distaste or greeted with misbegotten fantasies.

Pagan Religious Practices:
Orgiastic Worship and Sacred Prostitutes

The worship of Bacchus, the god of wine and fertility, of Cybele, the Mother Goddess, and of the gods of many of the mystery cults often took on an orgiastic character. Roman citizens were warned against such practices and at times forbidden by law to participate. Moralists complained that religion was being used as a cover for all sorts of licentious behavior.

The reenactment of the annual rebirth of vegetation and the hope for abundant fertility of cattle and wives dates back at least as far as the time of the Canaanites, who worshiped Baal and his consort Astarte on the tops of hills. Temple prostitutes in Babylonia perpetuated similar rites by engaging in sexual intercourse with priests and rulers of city-states. Select women were expected to spend the night in a room at the top of a tower in Babylon, satisfying the sexual desires of the god Marduk (or his earthly counterpart). According to Herodotus, a Greek traveler and writer, every woman was required to go to the temple of Ishtar in Babylon at least once in her lifetime and engage in sexual intercourse with a stranger.[1] This was regarded as a religious act, a sacrifice to the god or a fertility offering.[2]

Another form of sexual intercourse as ritual later emerged in the practice of the "holy weddings" within Gnostic worship. (Some Gnostics considered themselves Christians but held beliefs that church leaders regarded as heretical.) Finally this practice was abolished by Constantine, the first emperor to favor Christianity, in the fourth century after Christ.

In the time of Paul, the city of Corinth had become an infamous center of religious prostitution. The populous gave annual honors to the *hetairai*, prostitutes who dedicated themselves to the goddess Aphrodite. According to legend, the *hetairai* during the war with the Persians had persuaded the goddess to use her powers on behalf of the Greek soldiers, and for this act were held in high esteem in the centuries that followed. *Hetairai* in the Hellenized world were among the most educated of women (see chapter 1), well dressed and skillful in applying cosmetics and adorning themselves, often able to discuss philosophy and literature with their educated clientele. The freedom and status of the *hetairai* within Greek society often exceeded that of married women.

Another class of sacred prostitutes were little more than slaves owned by the temples. The Greek geographer Stabo of Amasia in Pontus, living in the first century before Christ, wrote that the temple of Aphrodite possessed more than one thousand slave prostitutes, both male and female, who were dedicated to the goddess and provided great wealth for the city. That lure for sailors, he added, is the basis for the proverb, "not for every man is the voyage into Corinth."[3]

In Rome, six women were selected as children to serve as Vestals, attending to the shrine of Vesta, and symbolizing the chastity of women in service of the goddess. Should a Vestal Virgin engage in sexual intercourse, her punishment would be burial alive. Meanwhile, the temples of Venus in Rome, like that of Aphrodite in Corinth, boasted of offering the services of slave prostitutes in honor of that goddess.[4]

Even Judaism had a history of sacred prostitution. Some interpret the sin of the sons of Eli, who engaged in intercourse with women who served at the tabernacle (1 Sam 2:22), as just such a practice. But certainly the office of cult prostitute was established within Judah and continued, in spite of attempts to eradicate it (1 Kings 15:12, 22:46), until the religious reform under King Josiah (2 Kings 14:21–24). The author of Deuteronomy recognized the practice existed, and declared that having sacred prostitutes within the land of Israel or even taking money so earned into the house of the Lord was an abomination (Deut. 23:17–18).

Now, among conservative Jews in the time of Paul, even social contacts between men and women were restricted. According to the Mishnah, a man might divorce his wife and not have to return her dowery if she were guilty of speaking to another man[5]; and even the act of speaking to a man in the street might be used as evidence of a bride's unfaithfulness to her intended.[6]

Because the Jews were well aware of the obscene orgiastic worship among their pagan neighbors and because the Jews were so concerned with potential contact between males and females, it is a wonder that women were allowed to be present with men during public worship at all. In practice, a compromise had been reached: women might be present during worship, but only if they were silent and out of sight (in a balcony or behind a curtain); women did not count in determining if a congregation were present for worship, for a minimum number consisted of a *minyan*, ten men; and although a woman might be qualified to participate in public worship by reading from Scripture, she was not allowed to "out of respect for the congregation."[7]

Paul's practice of having women and men together in worship and his approval of women as well as men leading in worship (which we shall examine more fully later on) must have shocked his Jewish and pagan contemporaries!

Jesus' Model of Respect for Women

Jesus set the example for his church. He taught both women and men (Matt. 14:21, 15:38), and he received praise from a woman who had heard him (Luke 11:27). Women were among his followers, making the long journeys on foot with the male disciples (Matt. 27:55; Luke 23:49, 55), and many of these women were mentioned by name in the Gospels. For example, Mark, writing several decades later about the crucifixion, recalled, "There were also women looking on from afar, among whom were Mary Magdalene, and Mary the mother of James the younger and of Joses, and Salome, who, when he was in Galilee, followed him, and served him; and also many other women who came up with him to Jerusalem" (Mark 15:40–41).

The gentle way Jesus reacted to a woman of ill repute who broke into a dinner party at the home of a Pharisee, sought Jesus out, anointed his feet with perfume, and wiped them with her hair, reflected his respect for the worth of women. As a startled hush fell over the party, Jesus turned to his critical host and told a parable that brought to everyone's attention the deep spiritual and moral yearning that had motivated this woman's actions (Luke 7:36–48). Moreover, Jesus' gentle chiding of Martha for her anxious concern in being a hostess and his praise of her sister Mary who sat at his feet and listened to his teachings (Luke 10:38–42) offer a living example of how Jesus welcomed women among his disciples (learners).

At times this value Jesus gave to women as disciples embarrassed his male followers. Once when Jesus was found talking to a woman of Samaria about her faith, his male disciples watched with guarded silence. "They marveled that he was speaking with a woman," recalled John, "but none said, 'What are you seeking?' or 'Why are you talking with her?'" (John 4:27).

Apparently, Jesus' example regarding women became the norm within the apostolic church. The apostles soon began to speak of the "women of our company" (Luke 24:22). When the apostles engaged in prayer, they did so "together with the women" (Acts 1:14). After the Day of Pentecost, "multitudes, both of men and women" were welcomed into the fellowship of believers (Acts 5:14), and both men and women were baptized (Acts 8:12).

Paul's Recognition of Women's Importance in the Church

Paul began as an enemy of this new following, actively seeking out Christians and imprisoning them in his zealousness to rid Jerusalem of such a heretical sect. The importance of the place of women in the Church is indicated by that fact that Paul (then Saul) arrested both men and women believers: "But Saul ravaged the church, entering house after house, dragging off both men and women and delivering them to prison" (Acts 8:3). Not content with limiting his attack to the city limits of Jerusalem, Paul (Saul) decided to pursue believers north to Damascus: "But Saul, still breathing threats and murder against the disciples of the Lord, approached the high priest and asked for letters to the synagogues in Damascus, so that if he found any belonging to the Way— both men and women— he might bring them bound to Jerusalem" (Acts 9:1–2).

Years later, Paul recalled how he had made no distinction between the sexes in his efforts to oppose Christianity, having "persectued this Way as far as to death, binding and delivering to prisons both men and women, as even the high priest and all the council of elders witness concerning me" (Acts 22:4–5). In the eyes of its enemies, the apostolic church included women who were just as dangerous in their heresy as the men, and Paul treated them alike. Since Paul began his relationship with Christianity by treating women and men the same, it seems unlikely that he would favor one over the other after his conversion. The same disregard for social restrictions of contact between men and women and the same abandoning of any protectionistic attitudes regarding women that characterized Paul's passion when he persecuted the Church continued to characterize Paul's passion when he became an apostle of the Church.

For example, when Paul, accompanied by Silas and Luke, first traveled to Europe, following a vision of a man pleading with Paul to bring the gospel message there also, they came to the city of Philippi and went to the riverbank. There they met some women and began telling them of the Christ. The first convert Paul made in Europe was Lydia, one of these women, whom he baptized (Acts 16:11–15). Paul's message continued to be aimed at both women and men, and wherever he preached, both sexes responded (for example, Acts 17:4, 11–12). Often the female believers are mentioned by name, another indication of their importance in the life of the Church. For example, in Athens among the number of men and women who believed in Paul's gospel, two individuals are remembered by name, a man named Dionysius and a woman named Damaris (Acts 17:34).

In Paul's letters, he acknowledged the value of women leaders within the churches. Some years after leaving Philippi, he wrote to the congregation there, entreating two women leaders, Euodia and Syntyche, to end a dispute between themselves. The fact that he named these women indicates their importance within the Church; moreover, he also described them as ones "who struggled beside me in the gospel, along with both Clement and the rest of my co-workers, whose names are in the book of life" (Phil. 4:2–3).

In Corinth, Paul lodged in the home of a Jewish couple, Prisca (Priscilla) and Aquila, who had been among the Jews exiled from Rome in A.D. 49. The church that developed in Corinth met in this couple's home (1 Cor. 16:19). Later, in another letter, Paul praised these two as "my co-workers in Christ Jesus, who risked their necks for my life, to whom not only I but also all the churches of the nations give thanks" (Rom. 16:3–4). It is interesting to note that Paul used the name Prisca, rather than its diminutive form Priscilla, in referring to her, and that in his greetings he placed her name before that of Aquila, her husband. Some assume he did so because she was more of a leader than her husband. Chrysostom, a fourth-century church leader, wrote that Prisca was a teacher of Apollos, pastor of the church in Corinth after Paul left.[8]

At the close of Paul's great treatise to the Romans, he listed a number of church leaders by name, persons worthy of his praise. Twenty-six persons are mentioned (including Prisca and Aquila), eight of whom are women. In fact, the list begins with Phoebe, whom Paul said "became a protectress of many and of myself as well" (Rom. 16:1–2). Phoebe, he pointed out, was a deacon of the church in Cenchreae. (Many translate the word as "deaconess," but the word itself is masculine, the same word used elsewhere in the New Testament for that office.) Chrysostom commented about both Phoebe and Prisca, "These were noble women, hindered in no way by their sex . . . and this is as might be expected, 'For in Christ Jesus there is neither male nor female.'"[9]

Among the other women praised in this closing portion of Romans is listed one about whom there is some mystery. In verse 7 Paul wrote, "Greet Andronicus and Junias my kindred and my co-prisoners, who are notable among the apostles, who indeed have been in Christ before me." Because the two names are in the accusative form (that is, they are recipients of the verb *greet*), the second name appears as *Junian*, which is the accusative form of the feminine name Junia. Because the two are listed as being notable among the apostles (that is, among missionaries—the general meaning of that word—not among the Twelve Apostles), some claim that both names therefore must be masculine and that Junian is a contraction of Junianus. Others soften the notion of a woman apostle by suggesting that Andronicus and Junia were a married couple, as were Aquila and Prisca, and that it was Andronicus who bore the honor of being referred to as a notable apostle, with Junia simply sharing his glory. Chrysostom, however, had no doubts regarding this person's sex or value, and he exclaimed, "Oh how great is the devotion of this woman, that she should be even counted worthy of the appellation of apostle!"[10]

Although Paul did not establish the practice of having women lead in worship alongside men, he certainly did approve of it.

On the Day of Pentecost, Peter told the crowds that had witnessed the miracle that what they had seen was a fulfillment of prophecy about the new age. Specifically, Peter quoted Joel 2:28–32, which begins, "And it shall be in the last days, says God, I will pour out my Spirit on all flesh, and your sons and your daughters shall prophesy, and your young men shall see visions and your old men shall dream dreams, and on my male slaves and on my female slaves in those days I shall pour out my Spirit and they shall prophesy" (Acts 2:17–18). The word *prophesy* means, simply, to speak for God. It may be speaking about the future (as the popular usage of the word denotes), but more often than that, it is speaking about the here and now. It is simply telling people what God wants them to hear. It is preaching that is inspired. And the sign of the new age, according to the prophet Joel and according to the apostle Peter, is the pouring out of God's Spirit so that both men and women, both young and old, both slave and free may speak for God.

It would be strange, indeed, if the Church under the apostles regarded this as a sign of the new age in Christ and yet forbade women the right to give inspired messages to the Church! And in fact it was not until later, after the age of the apostles, when the Greek attitude about women became dominant within the Church, that women were forbidden to preach.

Certainly, women exercised the gift of prophecy in the age of Paul. Besides Paul himself, seven men and four women are identified as prophets in the Book of Acts (Acts 11:27, 13:1, 15:32, 21:9,10). These women were the daughters of Philip, one of the original seven deacons of the church in Jerusalem (Acts 6:5). Paul referred to the act of women praying and prophesying during public worship, and he did so in a casual manner, as if such a practice were well established (1 Cor. 11:4–5). And in this same passage (1 Cor. 11), Paul made some remarkable statements about women, in the context of discussing the matter of head coverings during worship (which will be examined in chapter 5, this volume).

Paul's Letter to Corinth

In 1 Cor. 11:7, Paul wrote that woman is "the glory of man." He did so after stating that man is "the image and glory of God." At first reading, it sounds as if Paul were giving a backhanded compliment to women. But one must remember the opinions about women that he was attempting to change. Both Paul and his readers were aware of the traditional interpretation given to the account of the creation of Adam and Eve, which says, in essence, that God created Adam in God's image (forgetting that Gen. 1:27 states that God created both male and female in his image), doing so out of the dust of the earth; but God created Eve as an afterthought, out of the rib of the man. Therefore, Adam (and all men) are in the image of God, while Eve (and all women) are in the image of men, given to men that the race might continue. However, this interpretation goes, just as Eve led Adam away from God by tempting him, so women are a distraction to men in their pursuit of holiness. Hence, in God's wisdom the curse falls upon Eve and every women: "Your desire shall be for your husband, and he shall rule over you" (Gen. 3:16).

Such is the traditional use of the Genesis account to degrade women. Paul made four statements that contradict this interpretation. First, he stated that woman is the glory of man. She is not the distraction of men, as the Essenes claimed, nor an object to be owned and used, as the Greeks believed, but the very glory of man.

Second, in 1 Cor. 11:9, Paul reminded his readers that woman was created because man needs woman. The Authorized (King James) Version misses the force of the words in Greek. It reads simply, "Neither was the man created for the woman, but woman for the man." Many modern translations render Paul's words more accurately: "Neither was the man created for the sake of the woman, but the woman for the sake of the man." What Paul was unmistakably stating is that men need women. Women are not created just for the purpose of bearing and rearing children. Women are not simply the means by which men reproduce themselves. From the beginning man has needed woman. As God observed, "It is not good that man should be alone" (Gen. 2:18). Paul was reminding his Jewish readers that before God said that Eve's desire should be for her husband, Adam already needed Eve. And Paul was reminding his Gentile readers that the Stoic disdain for women is unrealistic and unnatural.

Third, Paul added in 1 Cor. 11:11, "Nevertheless, neither woman without man nor man without woman in the Lord."

Each needs the other. Paul was writing this in the context of discussing public worship. His words opposed the pagan practice of excluding women in worship and the synagogue practice of relegating women to a side chamber or a balcony as silent observers of the men at worship.

Then, in 1 Cor. 11:12, Paul made a further statement about the creation of Adam and Eve that topples the traditional interpretation. "For as the woman out of the man," his words read literally, "so also the man out of woman; but all things out of God." The old notion about women stated that they are inferior to men because Eve was created out of Adam. Paul observed that every man alive came out of woman (that is, was born of woman). The implication is that if Eve were inferior to Adam by virtue of being made out of his body, then every man is inferior to his mother for the same reason. In the last phrase, Paul added the reminder that all things are products of God's creation, alluding to the fact that just as God designed man, so God also designed woman.

A little further on in his letter to the church in Corinth, Paul made a statement to women that seems at first glance to contradict all he had written about women in worship up to this point: "As in all the churches of the saints, let the women in the churches be silent, for it is not permitted for them to speak. Instead, let them be silent, as the law says. But if they wish to learn anything, let them question their own husbands at home, for it is a shame for a woman to speak in church" (1 Cor. 14:33b–35). The translation of this passage, if taken quite literally and observed with all strictness, would mean that women are not to make any sound at all during worship. Women would not be allowed to sing during worship, either with the congregation or in a choir. No woman would be allowed to repeat the Lord's Prayer or recite a creed or read a responsive reading. When the worship bulletin called for a verbal expression in unison, only men would be permitted to read the words aloud. No woman could be employed to play an organ, for that would not be in keeping with the silence demanded of women. And no woman could make a verbal prayer request in times of crisis, nor greet a visitor, nor quiet a restless child. No woman would be permitted to cough, or to let her footsteps be heard as she crossed the room to be seated.

The traditional interpretation of these words of Paul's has not been so literal, of course. Instead, his words (as translated) have been employed to debar women from preaching, leading in worship, or even serving sacramental bread and wine (even when such actions do not involve any words spoken on the part of the server!). Such an interpretation is in keeping with Aristotle's words (quoting Sophocles) that "silence is a woman's glory."[11] But is it in keeping with what Paul actually wrote?

The context of this passage is public worship. More specifically, it is orderliness in public worship. Paul's central theme was "For God is not (a God) of confusion, but of peace" (1 Cor. 14:33a). The word that is usually translated "confusion" or sometimes "disorder"[12] is *akatastasia* (pronounced aka-tas-ta-SEE-a).

Paul once wrote how *akatastasia* was one of the things he had had to suffer from those who were hostile to the preaching of the gospel, along with afflictions, hardships, calamities, beatings, and imprisonments (2 Cor. 6:4b–5a). When Paul faced an unruly mob, he described their noisy confusion and disorder as *akatastasia*, which we translate "tumult." It is the same word that Jesus used to describe one of the signs of the coming destruction, in the phrase "wars and tumults" (Luke 21:9).

Now, Paul wrote to the church in Corinth that he did not want *akatastasia* in their public worship, for God is a God of peace. And in order to provide some orderliness to their worship, Paul gave them three sets of instructions: (1) only two persons, or at the most three, may speak in tongues, and then only if there are interpreters present (verses 27–28); (2) only two or three may prophesy, and they must take turns, each weighing the words of the others (verses 29–32); and (3) women are to be silent in church (verse 34a).

How could Paul acknowledge and approve of women praying and prophesying during public worship (chapter 11), and then a few pages later write that women must remain silent during public worship (chapter 14)? The answer to what at first glance seems to be a rude inconsistency lies in the choice of words Paul made when he penned those instructions—specifically the words translated "silence" and "speak."

For example, there is a word in Greek that means "tie shut," "muzzle." It is often used to describe a kind of forced silence, and perhaps it is best translated by our English idiom "shut up." This word is *phimoo* (fim-OH-o). It describes how Jesus' answer to their question silenced the Pharisees (Matt. 22:34). In the parable of the wedding feast, this word tells how the man who did not bother to wear a wedding garment remained speechless when confronted by the host (Matt. 22:12). Jesus used *phimoo* also as a command, to quiet the unclean spirit that he cast out of a man (Mark 1:25; Luke 4:35) and to still the raging wind and sea (Mark 4:39). *Phimoo* means forcing someone to be silent. When Paul wrote that women are to be silent, he did not use *phimoo*, even though the English translation might imply such a forceful command.

Another word for silence in Greek is a lovely word, *hesuchia* (hey-soo-KEY-ah), denoting quietness and stillness. Paul did instruct women to enter into *hesuchia*, in his first letter to Timothy (see chapter 4, this volume). But he instructed women to do so when they are studying. Paul did not use this word regarding women when they are worshiping.

Instead, Paul chose the Greek verb *sigao* (sig-AH-o) when he wrote, "Let the women in the churches be silent." Now, *sigao* is a voluntary silence. It was used to describe the decision of the disciples to remain silent about the transfiguration that they had just witnessed (Luke 9:36), and when Jesus told the Pharisees that if his disciples were silent (as the Pharisees insisted) then the very stones would cry out (Luke 19:40). It was used to describe Jesus' silence during his trial before Pilate (Mark 14:61), and the silence of the apostles and elders as they listened to a report by Paul and Barnabas when they returned from their missionary journey (Acts 15:12).

Sigao can also take the form of a request, as when the multitude accompanying Jesus told the insistent beggar to quit yelling (Luke 18:39), or when Peter motioned for the crowd to be silent (Acts 12:17).

Sigao is the kind of silence asked for in the midst of disorder and clamor. And Paul asked women of the Church to keep that kind of silence. Then Paul added, "It is a shame for a woman to speak in church" (verse 35b). How could Paul acknowledge and advocate women prophesying alongside men during worship and yet denounce women for speaking in church? Again, the answer lies in Paul's choice of words.

Greek has many words that can be translated "speak." Five of them denote preaching or proclaiming, and twenty-five others can be translated "say," "speak," or "teach." Some of them have various shades of meaning that can be reflected in the translation, but not all. But when Paul wrote that it is a shame for a woman to speak in church, his meaning can be seen if we look at which one of those thirty words he used.

He did not write that women are not to preach, or teach, or declare, or give a discourse, or proclaim, or affirm, or aver, or speak for something, or any other of the distinctive meanings found in many of those verbs. Instead, Paul wrote that women are not to *laleo* (la-LAY-o). Like the other verbs, *laleo* can denote the act of saying something quite important. But of all the verbs that can be translated "speak," only *laleo* can also mean, simply, "talk."

If someone wished to write in Greek the sentence "Please do not talk during the prayers," the verb would have to be *laleo*. And since Paul's instructions were given to a congregation troubled with tumult and discord during the worship services, he told the women not to *laleo*—that is, not to converse. Paul was telling them that it is shameful for women to keep talking during the worship service.

Why would Paul aim this directive toward women, rather than toward both men and women? The social roles, especially of married women, may suggest an answer. Kari Torjesen Malcolm, who served as a missionary in China as her parents had done, offers a living example of the situation in Corinth that led Paul to instruct the women in that church to keep silent and not converse:

My mother used to compare the situation in Corinth to the one she and my father faced in northern China. Back in the 1920s when they were first to bring God's message to that forgotten area, they found women with bound feet who seldom left their homes and who, unlike the men, had never in their whole lives attended a public meeting or a class. They had never been told as little girls, "Now you must sit still and listen to the teacher." Their only concept of an assembly was a family feast where everyone talked at once.

When these women came to my parents' church and gathered on the women's side of the sanctuary, they thought this was a chance to catch up on the news with their neighbors and to ask questions about the story of Jesus they were hearing. Needless to say, along with babies crying and toddlers running about, the women's section got rather noisy! Add to that the temptation for the women to shout questions to their husbands across the aisle, and you can imagine the chaos. As my mother patiently tried to tell the women that they should listen first and chitchat or ask questions later, she would mutter under her breath, "Just like Corinth; it just couldn't be more like Corinth."[13]

Paul approved of women praying and prophesying during worship. He insisted that men and women should be together, and that in Christ they are one. But these were new and radical ideas to both Jew and Gentile. In practice, sexual equality among Christians led to a disregard for orderliness and courtesy during worship, especially on the part of women who were unaccustomed to listening to public speakers or to participating in public worship. To such women, Paul said, "Hush up."

Paul also told such women to "be subject" during the worship. He used the same word as in his famous discourse on the relationship of husbands and wives (Eph. 5:21–22), *hupotasso-*

mai. Actually, he used this word twice. First, when Paul instructed those who would prophesy to take turns, he anticipated that his instructions would be met with an objection something like this: "If the Spirit inspires me to speak, how can I hold back the words until someone else finishes speaking?" Paul's answer was simple: it is only by taking turns that all can listen to all who would prophesy and thereby all can learn and all can be encouraged (verse 31); moreover, "the spirits of the prophets are subject to the prophets" (verse 32). Then, when Paul told women not to talk during the worship service, he made the appeal, "Let them be subject, as also the laws says" (verse 34).

This last phrase, "as also the law says," has confused scholars. Some translators print *law* with a capital *L*, as if *the law* here referred to the Law of Moses. But nowhere in the Old Testament is there any command for women to remain silent during worship. Nor is there any such law known to have existed in Corinth or any other pagan city. Some Bibles have a cross-reference to 1 Tim. 2:11, but that passage could not be the law to which Paul makes reference, since when he wrote to the Corinthians, he had yet to write to Timothy!

There is one law, however, to which Paul could rightly appeal, and which his readers would recognize. English-speaking readers who find *hupotassomai* rendered as "be subject to" might expect any law referred to, to be a legal code in some book, enforced by some authorities who throw offenders in prison. But *hupotassomai* is a voluntary attitude of being responsive to the needs of others (see chapter 2, this volume). The spirits of the prophets are "subject" to the willingness of the prophets to take turns in speaking. So also let the women be quiet, "subject" to the needs of all to hear those who are leading in worship. The law, then, to which Paul makes an appeal is the law of love (*agape*) and the code is the Golden Rule.

In a situation where worship was tumultuous with the chattering of women unaccustomed to listening quietly to others,

Paul was simply applying a principle he wrote in his letter to the Ephesians; "Be subject (*hupotassomai*) to one another, out of reverence for Christ" (Eph. 5:21).

Questions for Thought and Discussion

1. Why do you suppose religion and prostitution were joined together at times in the ancient world? Are there more recent examples of sexual attraction being associated with religious fervor?

2. What do you suppose Jesus' critics said about the fact that he included women among his disciples?

3. Before Paul's conversion, when he persecuted Christians, he treated both male and female believers alike. Was this fair, considering the way his society treated them differently?

4. If it is a sign of the new age that both men and women shall prophesy, why do you suppose some churches do not allow women to preach?

5. Paul declared that man needs woman, and that woman is the glory of man. In what ways are these statements true today?

6. Imagine a worship service in which women literally kept silence, making no noise at all. What changes would this make in worship?

7. Paul told women who had questions during worship to wait and ask their husbands at home. What would be the advantages of this for the church? For the women? For their husbands? The disadvantages?

4. Educating Women

Some biblical scholars doubt that the apostle Paul wrote the two letters to Timothy and the letter to Titus, even though these epistles are contained within the New Testament and state that they are from Paul.

Why would some question their authorship? The churches described in these letters seem to be highly organized, more so than one would expect to find during the lifetime of the apostles. For example, Paul's practice in establishing churches was to train elders to oversee the congregations after he left, and often deacons were selected to serve the needs of the growing churches as well. Later, after the age of the apostles, the office of bishop was formed, providing ecclesiastical overseers for groups of churches. In these three letters, references are made to deacons (1 Tim. 3:8–13), elders (1 Tim. 5:1, 17–19; Titus 1:5–7), and bishops (1 Tim. 3:1–7; Titus 1:7–16). The elders were even given salaries (1 Tim. 5:17–18). Moreover, the beginning of an important order of widows that became prominent later on in the early church is mentioned. (1 Tim. 5:2–16)

In addition, the language within these three letters differs somewhat in style from that of the other letters from Paul, a fact that is more apparent in the Greek than in an English translation. And more than one-third of the words used in these epistles (excluding names) are used nowhere else in Paul's writings.

Therefore, a number of scholars suspect that these letters were penned by another person, using Paul's great name. Today we would regard such an action as deceptive and dishonest, but in the ancient world it was fairly common for someone who was writing something in the spirit of a great teacher or statesman to use that person's name.

Another point in which these letters seemingly are distinct from Paul's other writings is the attitude they reflect regarding women. For example, the Authorized (King James) Version of 1 Tim. 2:11–13 reads, "Let the woman learn in silence with all subjection. But I suffer not a woman to teach, nor to usurp authority over the man, but to be in silence. For Adam was first formed, then Eve. And Adam was not deceived, but the woman being deceived was in the transgression. Notwithstanding she shall be saved in childbearing, if they continue in faith and charity and holiness with sobriety." At first glance, one might certainly conclude that Paul could not have been the author of this passage. It appears to uphold the traditional interpretation of the story of Eden, that Adam was superior to Eve because he was made first and because she was the first to fall to temptation.

Elsewhere, Paul carefully balanced the notion that Eve was inferior to Adam because she was made out of Adam's rib and because she was made after Adam with the fact that Eve was made because Adam needed her and that all men are born "out of" women (1 Cor. 11:8–9, 11–12; see chapter 3, this volume). Also, elsewhere Paul wrote of the fall of mankind as Adam's sin—not Eve's—and how death came through that man (Rom. 5:14; 1 Cor. 15:21–22). Not only that, but this passage in 1 Timothy (as translated) states that a woman will be saved by having children (providing they are steadfast in faith, love, holiness, and sobriety). This idea of salvation through childbearing is a radical departure from Paul's famous and often-repeated theme of salvation through faith! Was Paul saying that men are saved by God's grace, but women only by producing good children?

One thing is certain: a closer look at this passage in 1 Timothy reveals a complex message about women that is difficult to translate. A very literal, word-for-word translation sounds confusing (and is). It reads this way: "Let a woman learn in silence in all subjection; but I do not permit a woman to teach nor to exercise authority of (over) a man, but to be in silence. For Adam was formed first, then Eve. And Adam was not deceived, but the woman, being utterly deceived, has become in transgression; but she will be saved through the childbearing, if they remain in faith and love and sanctification with good moral judgment."

One quick and easy way to avoid a close study of this teaching is to dismiss the whole letter as spurious, written by someone other than Paul, the champion of equality of men and women in Christ. But in spite of the serious questions raised concerning the authorship of 1 and 2 Timothy and Titus, there are some very sound reasons for concluding that Paul really did write these letters. If so, then how can this passage be reconciled with Paul's assertions elsewhere about women as coworkers with him, noted among the apostles, important to the Church as prophets, one with men in Christ Jesus? To answer this question, we must look at the nature of the letters to Timothy, then at the meanings of the words themselves, and finally at the possible interpretations that make sense of what is written.

The Nature of the Letters to Timothy

1 Timothy is, above all else, a personal letter, addressed to a young minister whom Paul lovingly called "my true child in the faith" (1 Tim. 1:2a)[8]. Not only was this letter (like 2 Timothy and Titus) speaking to a specific dear friend in Christ, it was also written about a specific situation within a beloved congregation. Paul was asking Timothy to remain with the church at Ephesus (one of the churches founded by Paul, and the one with which he remained the longest of any during his missionary journeys). Problems within that church concerned Paul. Someone was teaching a different doctrine to that body of Christians (1 Tim. 1:3, 4:1), and the congregation was suffering from angry arguments (1 Tim. 2:8). Some persons had rejected conscience, and Paul named two of them as guilty of blasphemy (1 Tim. 1:19–20, 4:2).

Because the letter was personal, addressing problems known to both the writer and the recipient, the situation in that church was not fully described. There was no need for Paul to waste time relating to Timothy what he already knew quite well. So a modern reader finds it difficult to get a clear understanding of the meaning of Paul's words. It is like listening to snatches of one end of a conversation, and then trying to make sense of what is heard.

Letting Women Learn

Concerning the question of educating women in the Church, however, much is known. Whenever Paul established a church, he insisted that women were to be educated in the faith. He began this passage in 1 Timothy with the words "let a woman learn," and while such a program would be in keeping with Paul's goal for women, it was at variance with Jewish and Greek customs.

Jewish women were not included in formal education. It was permissible for a man to teach Scripture to both boys and girls,[1] but a woman could not teach even the youngest of children in a school, and one rabbi said that "if a man gives his daughter a knowledge of the Law, it is as though he taught her lechery."[2]

Women were to be educated only in matters regarding homemaking skills. As one rabbi said, "There is no wisdom in woman except with the distaff."[13a] (See chapter 1, this volume.)

Just a few years before Paul's death, Joshua ben Gamala instituted a law that teachers should be appointed in every province and in every town, that all Jewish children above the age of six or seven might be placed in their care. But this introduction of compulsory education excluded girls. Greek women, likewise, were not educated, except in the arts of homemaking.

Therefore, Paul's desire that women be educated in the faith was both radical in thought and difficult in execution. Women were not used to listening to lectures or thinking about theological concepts, or studying at all. Normally bound to the solitude of home or limited in social contact to their own husbands and children, these women had an opportunity to visit with one another in classroom settings. Therefore Paul instructed that women are to learn, but "in silence with all subjection" (1 Tim. 2:11). The word for subjection is the noun form of *hupotassomai*, which, as noted already, is the voluntary willingness to be responsive to the needs of others (in this case, to the needs of others to listen, of themselves to hear, and of the teachers to communicate without noisy competition). Just as in worship (1 Cor. 14), so in study: women are to be considerate of others and quick to hear the words of the leaders. But the word for silence is a lovely word, *hesuchia* (hey-soo-KEY-ah). It does not mean simply refraining from talking. It means restful quietness, as in meditation or study. A few sentences before, Paul used this same word to describe the peaceful and quiet life (1 Tim. 2:2), good and acceptable before God, the kind of life Paul wished for all believers.[4]

The difference between being quiet in order to hear someone speak (*sigao*—see chapter 3) and being quiet in order to listen with studious attention (*hesuchia*)is well illustrated in Acts 21:40 to 22:2. At the temple in Jerusalem, Paul was facing a hostile mob that was clamoring in such an uproar that the Roman tribune came with soldiers and centurions to establish order. The tribune had Paul arrested. But when Paul spoke to him in Greek, asking for an opportunity to address the crowd, the surprised official gave him permission. So Paul motioned to the people with his hand, and a great silence (*sige*, the noun form of *sigao*) fell over the crowd. Then, when Paul addressed them in the Hebrew language, we read that the people showed *hesuchia*. At his signal, they became still; as he spoke, they became quietly attentive. Paul was asking the same of women. He was telling women that they must learn, and to do so they must be quiet and respectful.

Providing education for women, however, must have incited considerable criticism from family members and community leaders outside the Church. Any change creates resistence, but the matter of educating women ran the risk of moral censure from non-Christians.

Teachers, at first, had to be men, for only men were educated in the faith. And Jewish custom strictly forbade women from conversing with men other than their husbands.[5] Moreover, the Jewish sages declared that any man who spends too much time talking with women "will inherit Gehenna" (hell).[6] Any man who taught Jewish women in the Church might be accused by their husbands of trying to break up marriages, or might be told that he was going to hell for his efforts.

Greeks, when associating women with religion, would think of the temple of Diana in Ephesus, which had hundreds of prostitutes, called *Melissai* (bees). Any man who taught Greek women in the Church might be accused of catering to sacred prostitutes, or of seeking to entice women to enter into this position within this new Eastern religion.

Because of the potential scandals that might arise, unfairly, in an attempt to educate women in the Church, Paul urged Christian women to dress modestly and adorn themselves with good deeds (1 Tim. 2:9–10; see chapter 5, this volume). He also prohibited women from teaching men (a role that would have infuriated men in that society) and from exercising authority over men. This latter phrase is one translation of a strange word, *authenteo* (au-then-TEH-o). It appears nowhere else in the New Testament. At one time this word described one who kills with his own hands (himself or another). Later, it was used to indicate how one may act on his or her own authority, and dominate others in an autocratic manner. "Domineer" may be a good translation of *authenteo*.

It is the opposite of the kind of spirit Paul commended to all Christians, of love and respect. It is quite possible that Paul had in mind a certain woman or group of women in Ephesus when he wrote this passage. If so, Paul was not willing to lessen his insistence that women are to learn, in spite of the high-handed attitude of one or some. Instead, he wrote that they are to learn in quietness, without being rude or domineering.

Adam and Eve Revisited

Paul then made three statements about Adam and Eve: (1) Adam was formed first, before Eve; (2) Adam was not deceived, but Eve was utterly deceived; (3) Eve became "in transgression." Why would Paul suddenly introduce the subject of the first couple, and why would he feel it was important to state these three points?

As has already been noted, some teachers of false doctrines were troubling the congregation at Ephesus. The nature of these teachings can only be inferred from Paul's objections to them, but based on his concern about such a rising heresy, it seems certain that the statements about Adam and Eve were designed to contravert such false teachings.

What was the teaching that troubled Paul? It was characterized by useless speculations and the desire for controversy (1 Tim. 1:4, 6:4; 2 Tim. 2:23), a denigration of marriage and a demand for dietary abstinence (1 Tim. 4:3), immoral practices (1 Tim. 4:2), great attention given to genealogies and myths (1 Tim. 1:4, 4:7; compare Titus 1:14, 3:9), and a denial of the resurrection of the body (2 Tim. 2:18). This list fits one heresy: Gnosticism. The basic thought of Gnosticism is that matter is inherently evil and spirit is good. Therefore, the Creator of this physical world must be evil. The Gnostics taught that there is a good God, who created a series of emanations (called aeons), each one farther from God than the previous one, each one more evil than those before it until at last there was one who created this material world. If a person is to reach God, then he or she must learn the names of these emanations, know the passwords and means of getting around them, farther and farther up the ladder, until at last reaching—through this secret knowledge (*gnosis*)—the presence of the prime Deity. It is quite possible that by "genealogies" Paul was referring to the mythical series of emanations a Gnostic was told he or she must transverse in order to arrive at the true Spirit.

Moreover, if the physical is evil, then our bodies too are evil. Some Gnostics taught that this means one must deny one's body and any physical pleasures and turn away from base desires. (Hence, one must not eat food that is especially appetizing, and one must abstain from sexual satisfaction and refrain from marriage; one Gnostic taught that marriage was of the old covenant, but in this new age no one who marries can inherit the kingdom of God.) However, other Gnostics taught that since matter and spirit are opposites, one's body cannot affect one's spirit and therefore the physical desires and lusts are to be gratified and stated without regard to senseless restrictions or conventional morality. (Hence, the Gnostics who concurred with this notion disdained any inhibiting conscience and engaged in any kind of pleasureable practices.) All Gnostics, of course, rejected the teaching of the resurrection of one's body.

It is almost certain that the false teachings in Ephesus that concerned Paul were those of Gnosticism.

Now, a great portion of the Gnostic writings added to or rewrote the story of Adam and Eve, often teaching that the first man was androgynous (both male and female) until he/she was cut in two, with Adam and Eve (who was to Adam "bone of my bone and flesh of my flesh") then becoming separate individuals. In some accounts, Eve was created before Adam or else was the spiritual force who awakened Adam and resided in the Tree of Life.[7] The physical Eve, following the words of the "instructor," ate of the fruit of the tree and gave the fruit to her husband, and both received knowledge—which was good.[8] Other Gnostic writings depict Adam as not understanding what is happening.[9]

While it is not known which form of Gnosticism was represented at Ephesus, Paul's declarations about Adam and Eve opposed all such myths. Adam was formed first, Paul wrote, and then Eve. The traditional interpretation of this sequence of creation is that women are inferior to men, since Adam was God's original design while Eve was an afterthought. Since in this passage Paul recited the order of the creation of the first human couple, it has been assumed that Paul was thereby reaffirming this traditional interpretation. But Paul avoided mention of this interpretation. Within the context, it seems almost certain that Paul's intention was not to make any statement regarding superiority or inferiority, but to refute the doctrines of certain Gnostic teachers.

Paul added that Eve was utterly deceived (the word means "cheated" or "tricked") while Adam was not deceived. Some Gnostic teachings would have Adam ignorant and Eve informed of the truth of the fruit of the Tree of Knowledge (*Gnosis*).[10] Paul laid the responsibility upon Adam rather than Eve (contrary to the traditional interpretation, which has Eve—as all women since that time—tempting Adam and therefore becoming the source of humankind's downfall and misery). However, Paul also stated that Eve became "in transgression" (that is violating the law of God). Many Gnostics would lay no blame on Eve, seeing the so-called fall as really humankind's great leap forward in grasping knowledge and finding enlightenment.

The Question of Salvation for Women

Then Paul added a peculiar sentence: "But she will be saved through the childbearing, if they remain in faith and love and sanctification with good moral judgment" (1 Tim. 2:15). Some translators begin this sentence with "but women will be saved" or "but woman will be saved," and then continue, "if she remains in faith. . . ." They change the wording in an attempt to make sense of a confusing statement. However, in the Greek, it reads "but she will be saved . . . if they remain"—but who is "she" and who are "they"?

Several possibilities have been suggested.

"She" might refer to Eve. If so, then Paul was saying that Eve, the mother of humanity, will be saved not by faith and righteousness (she was deceived and she transgressed), but by her childbearing, if they (her descendants) remain in faith and love and sanctification (the means of salvation through Christ, as Paul preached).

Or "she" might refer to someone known to Paul and Timothy, who, like Eve, had been deceived and had become "in transgression" with God. And just as Paul once wrote how a believer might someday save his or her spouse (1 Cor. 7:16), so this woman might someday be saved by her believing children.

Or "she" might refer to any woman in general. If so, then what does Paul's teaching about childbearing and "they" mean? It might be read to mean that a woman is saved in the grand gift of being a mother. But this notion would run contrary to Paul's gospel, that "by grace you are saved through faith . . . not because of works, lest any man should boast" (Eph. 2:8). Could Paul have failed to apply this same teaching to women and to conclude that women are saved by grace through faith, and not because of giving birth, lest any mother should boast? Furthermore, the last phrase makes a mother's salvation depend upon the faith of her children, something which, ultimately, is out of her control and up to them.

Paul's words can also mean that a woman ("she") will be saved during giving birth (in an age when it was not uncommon for a woman to die during delivery) if she and her husband ("they") have faith, love, and sanctification. Paul might have been recalling that the curse upon Eve specified that she would have to bear great pain in giving birth, and thus he might have been writing that women who have faith are not to be anxious for their lives during that painful time.

Moreover, if "she" refers to womankind in general, there is yet another possible interpretation. "The childbearing" might not refer to giving birth in general, but to the specific birth of the Christ child. If so, then Paul was saying in effect, "You who regard women as spiritually inferior because of the example of Eve, remember that when God provided a means of salvation for us all, he did so through the cooperation of a woman, Mary. And you Gnostics who regard the physical as evil, my gospel tells me that my Redeemer was born of a woman, flesh and blood born of flesh and blood, and that by this means the good news of salvation is offered to all who have faith and love and sanctification."

Which of these interpretations is closest to what Paul had in mind as he penned the words? No one can be certain.

Several certainties regarding this passage can be arrived at, however. First, Paul favored education for women, regardless of the difficulties in providing it. In his second letter to Timothy, he complained of how there were persons "creeping into houses and capturing silly women," women who were "heaped with sins, led by various lusts, always learning and never being able to come to a full knowledge of truth" (2 Tim. 3:6–7). But in the face of such a threat to women, Paul insisted that women be provided with the opportunity to learn.

Second, Paul insisted that salvation is for women, and that through childbirth salvation is made possible—whether he meant the birth of Christ or the birth of those who would learn to receive Christ in faith. Either way, woman is essential to God's gift of life and life eternal.

And third, Paul concluded with the essential elements of salvation: faith, love, and sanctification. He added that this last element, sanctification (being set apart in God's love) is to be accompanied with *sophrosune* (so-fro-SOON-ay). It means good judgment, especially in terms of moral decisions, the very quality that Eve lacked and that Paul would now commend to women and those born of women who live in faith.

Questions for Thought and Discussion

1. Paul wanted the churches to be coeducational. What would his critics most likely have said about this? What reasons would they have given?
2. Which interpretation do you favor of the teachings "but she will be saved through childbearing, if they remain in faith and love and sanctification with good moral judgment"?

3. Some Gnostics believed that the material world is evil and our bodies are prisons of our souls; therefore, we must deny ourselves physical satisfactions and pleasures. Is that attitude still held by some people today? Why or why not?

4. Other Gnostics believed that our souls are not effected by what we do with our bodies, so we might as well gratify our desires and embrace physical pleasures. Does that belief have any modern counterpart? If so, how is this belief defended today?

5. The Gnostics believed that knowledge is good, and that it was right for Adam and Eve to desire the fruit of the tree of knowledge of good and evil. How would you respond to this Gnostic viewpoint?

6. Paul wrote that Eve was "utterly deceived" and yet that she became "in transgression." What was she deceived about? How could she be guilty if she were deceived?

5. The Question of Dress and Hairstyles

Paul faced a problem. He envisioned a unity between Jews and Gentiles through a common faith in Christ. In the Church, Jewish Christians and Gentile Christians, slaves and masters, women and men, would all be equal. But in his grand attempt to make this dream come true, Paul found an obstacle that had to be removed: the different meanings given to head coverings and hair lengths and styles.

For Jews, worshiping without one's head covered was regarded with stern disapproval. Jewish men recited each morning the prayer "Blessed be Thou, O God, Who crowns Israel with beauty." They believed that the Shekhinah, the glory and radiance of the Almighty, surrounds the worshiper and rests upon the man and woman who please God. Therefore, it was regarded as an act of reverence and humility for a person to wear a head covering during worship, just as Moses wore a veil after descending Mount Sinai to hide the radiance of his face after being near God (Exod. 34:29-35). Some people wore something on their heads at all times, whether awake or asleep.

Jewish women were required to wear their hair bound up whenever they left their homes. Unbound, flowing hair was regarded as sensual and almost a form of nudity. If a woman let her hair down in public she was seen as tempting men to sin. Therefore, the Mishnah declared that a husband might divorce his wife and not have to return her dowry in the event that she "goes out with her hair unbound . . . or speaks to any man."[1] Men might let their hair grow long, but they were under no such compulsion to tie up their locks. "How does a man differ from a woman?" the Mishnah asks. "He may go with hair unbound and with garments rent, but she may not go with hair unbound and with garments rent."[2]

Some Jewish women would refrain from letting their hair down even in the privacy of their own homes, choosing instead to wear a head covering at all times. The Jewish Talmud tells of a high priest who was accidentally defiled on the Day of Atonement and therefore was prevented from officiating. When his brother officiated in his stead, their mother bragged that she saw two high priests in one day. When wise men asked her what she had done to merit such, she answered, "Throughout the days of my life the beams of my house have not seen the plaits of my hair."[3] (The wise men observed, however, that many other women did likewise without receiving such an honor.)

Modern Christians sometimes suppose that Jewish women of the Bible days were required to wear veils across their faces. Although this practice may have appeared from time to time, a veil was not required as a sign of modesty or humility. In fact, in the Old Testament a face veil may have been a sign of a prostitute, as indicated by the following story.

In the age of the Hebrew patriarchs, it was a law that if a woman were widowed without children, her deceased husband's brother would be obligated to take her into his house and provide her with a son, who would maintain the family line and inherit the deceased man's property. This arrangement was known as the law of levirate marriage. Judah, one of the twelve sons of Jacob, himself had three sons, Er, Onan, and Shelah. Er married a woman named Tamar, and he died without issue. Judah therefore provided Onan to Tamar, but he too died without issue. Judah feared giving his last son, Shelah, to Tamar, thinking that he too might perish. So Judah put her off, year after year. At last, after Judah himself was widowed, Tamar decided to bear an heir by tricking Judah himself into fathering her son. When Judah traveled to a nearby city, Tamar put off her mourning clothes and wore normal garments, and also she wore a veil across her face. Then she sat at the city gate and waited for Judah. When he saw her, "he thought her to be a harlot, for she had covered her face" (Gen. 38:15). So he propositioned her, and through this ruse Tamar became pregnant with twin sons of the lineage of Judah. This story indicates that veils at the time of Judah were symbols of prostitution among the Hebrews.

The words used in the Old Testament to describe women's clothing are not well understood, especially regarding head coverings. The Assyrian artist's portrayal of the destruction of the Judean city of Lachish shows Jewish women wearing long strips of cloth over their heads, like shawls that hung down behind them to the length of their hemlines. None of these women were pictured wearing veils.

What we know about Gentile styles is the following. During the classical period in Greece, wives wore scarves similar to those of the women of Lachish, long enough so that the Greek matrons could wrap one end of the cloth around their faces, hiding all but their eyes and foreheads when appearing in public places. By the time of Paul, men of Hellenized culture wore their hair relatively short. As Ovid (43 B.C.–A.D. 17), a Roman poet, advised young men in *The Art of Love*, "Don't let your hair grow long, and when you visit a barber, patronize only the best. Don't let him mangle your beard."[4] Greek girls wore long hair, and matrons wore their hair bound up on their heads in braids or with hair pins. Prostitutes, however (other than the sophisticated *hetairai* who served as courtesans of the wealthy), wore their hair quite short, often clipped closer than that of their male customers. Greek men would have found the Jewish insistence upon wearing head coverings during worship strange if not distasteful.

Paul's Instructions Regarding Hair and Head Coverings

In attempting to unify both Gentile and Jewish believers into one church, Paul felt the need to address the question of head coverings and hairstyles. In 1 Corinthians, he wrote specific instructions in an attempt to uphold one central principle: "Be without offense both to Jews and to Greeks and to the church of God, as I also in all things please all, not seeking my own advantage, but that of the many, in order that they may be saved" (1 Cor. 10:32). Paul wanted his readers to accommodate themselves to practices that would not offend either Jewish or Gentile believers.

Paul then immediately entered into the matter of head coverings and hairstyles. A literal translation of this passage into English discloses how confusing Paul's words are:

But I praise you because you have remembered all things of me and you hold fast to you the traditions as I delivered to you. But I wish you to know that Christ is the head of every man, and head of a wife, the husband, and head of Christ, God. Every man praying or prophesying (while) having (anything) down over (his) head shames the head of him. But, every women praying or prophesying with the head uncovered shames the head of her, for it is one and the same thing with the woman who has been shaved. For if a woman is not covered, let her be shorn; but if (it is) ugly for a woman to be shorn or to be shaved, let her be covered. For a man indeed is obligated not to be covered, the head being the image and glory of God; but the wife is glory of husband. For man is not from woman, but woman because of the man. Therefore the woman ought to have authority on the head because of the angels. Nevertheless, neither woman separate from man nor man separate from woman in (the) Lord, for as the woman from the man, so also the man through the woman; but all things of God. Among you yourselves judge: is it fitting, a woman to pray to God uncovered? (Does) not nature itself teach you that a man indeed if he wears his hair long, it is a dishonor to him, but a woman, if she wears her hair long, it is a glory to her? The long hair has been given to her instead of a covering. (1 Cor. 11:2–15)

Traditionally, this passage has been interpreted to mean that men are required to wear their hair short (in fact, the medieval practice of priests having their pates plucked bare—tonsured— was an overzealous application of this scripture) and keep their heads uncovered during worship, while women are to cover their heads during worship. Moreover, this passage has been interpreted to justify the notion that women, while they have souls, are by nature between men and animals in terms of powers of reason, ethical understanding, and theological insights. (After all, man is the glory of God, while woman is the glory of man.) This led in turn to a denial of education to women during the Middle Ages.

As has been noted already in chapter 3, a closer look at Paul's actual words affirms rather than debases women. The apostle rejected the idea of the inferiority of women to men that had been based on the story of Adam and Eve. Paul pointed out that Eve was created because Adam was incomplete without her, and that the wife is the glory of her husband. He also added that while Eve was taken out of Adam's side, every man since then has come from his mother's body. And so he summarized the question this way: "Neither woman separate from man nor man separate from woman in the Lord," for all things are from God. Men and women are not to be separate during worship—both men and women are to lead in worship by praying and prophesying.

But what about prohibitions and customs regarding head coverings and hairstyles?

A Closer Look at Paul's Solution

In order to understand Paul's solution to the problem, one must be introduced to the meaning of several key words in this passage.

For example, the Greek words for man and woman also mean "husband" and "wife." This was not Paul's choosing, but is inherent in the Greek language. Paul could have chosen words meaning "male" and "female" when he intended to indicate persons of each sex who are not necessarily married, but these words in Greek connote more than Paul wanted to say and they would have misled his readers. So in this passage (as in many New Testament writings) the decision whether to translate one word "husband" or "man" and the other "wife" or "woman" is determined by their context. In the literal translation given ear-lier, the words are translated "husband" and "wife" only when one can be fairly certain that Paul was referring to married cou-ples.

The word Paul used in this passage for head is *kephale* (kef-ah-LAY), and not *arche* (ar-KAY). As was noted in chapter 3, *arche* means "beginning," "boss," or "chief," while *kephale* means "physical head," or, figuratively, "one who proceeds an-other into battle." Although Paul did describe Christ as *arche* of the Church in Col. 1:18, in this passage whenever "head" ap-pears, it is a translation of *kephale*.

"Shorn" translates a form of the verb *keiro* (KY-roe), which means "shear" (as, a sheep) or "cut short" (as one's hair).

"Covered" is the verb *katakalupto* (kata-ka-LOOP-toe), which is used nowhere else in the New Testament. Elsewhere, *kalupto* (ka-LOOP-toe) is used to mean "cover," "hide," or "conceal." When Paul added the preposition *kata* to the verb, he was de-liberately altering its meaning from just "cover" to "cover down over." In verse 4, when Paul spoke of a man praying or pro-phesying with something down over his head, he used the same preposition, *kata* (ka-TAH), "down over." Now, at all other times in the New Testament, including the writings of Paul, when something is said to be "on" someone's head, the prepo-sition *epi* (eh-PEE) was used. Only here did Paul write of some-thing being *kata*, "down over," one's head. Some translators render *katakalupto* as "wearing a veil." If veil implies a face cov-ering, then such a translation is misleading.

"Hair" in Greek is *thrix*, but Paul, in this passage, chose a different word, *kome* (KOH-mee). It too is used nowhere else in the New Testament. It does not mean, simply, "hair." Rather, it denotes hair that is long and ornamental.[5]

"Nature," which Paul said teaches that long hair on a man is dishonorable, is *phusis* (FOO-sis). It means "nature" and "the natural order," but it also can be used to describe a mode of feeling or acting that is almost instinctive because of long habit. In that sense, *phusis* means "long-established custom."

What, then, was Paul saying?

He began by referring to the "tradition" that he had already delivered to the church in Corinth. This may mean the gospel, but usually Paul used the word we translate "gospel" when he meant the good news of Christ. It is much more likely that by "tradition" Paul was reminding church members of teachings and interpretations he gave to them concerning how they could apply the gospel to their daily lives.

Some of his teachings were delivered to that church in the letter we now know as 2 Corinthians. Careful study of both letters has led most scholars to conclude with confidence that 2 Corinthians was written before 1 Corinthians. Thus, the order of the two in our Bible does not reflect the order in which they were written.

In 2 Cor. 3:7–18, Paul referred to the veil that Moses put over his face after descending from Mt. Sinai because his skin shone with a brightness that frightened the Israelites (Exod. 34:29–35). Paul remarked that this glory on Moses faded, just as the splendor of the old covenant through Moses had faded away. Now, Paul declared, the new covenant we have through Christ is of greater splendor, for this covenant is permanent.

The Jewish custom of wearing head coverings during worship was linked to the idea of God's radiance (Shekhinah) shining upon the devout. Just as one might wear a hat to keep off the sun's rays, one would wear a hat when entering the brilliance of God's splendor. The custom of wearing something on top of one's head became a symbol of the kind of glory that Moses covered with a veil. The head covering in Paul's day was usually a prayer shawl, the *tallit*, which would hang down from the devout man's or woman's head.

Now, in 1 Corinthians Paul gave a theological reason why a Christian man ought not to wear something hanging down from the head while praying or prophesying. He began by reminding his readers that their head is not Moses, but Christ. His next sentences imply that what one does with one's head makes a theological statement about Christ. To cover one's head, Paul seems to be saying, is to act as if one were ashamed of Christ, our head, who is the image and glory of God. The question is not what a man does with his head, but what a man says by what he does with his head.

Jewish custom demanded that women too cover their heads when worshiping. If Paul wished to be consistent in his insistence on the oneness of men and women in Christ, one would expect him to offer the same instructions to women concerning head coverings as he did to men. But what a woman did with her head held different social significance from what a man did with his.

Married Jewish women were obligated to keep their hair bound up on their heads or else covered over whenever they appeared in public—as was the practice of many Greek matrons, as well. It was a symbol of their married state, much like a wedding ring today. For a Jewish woman to loosen her hair in public would have been even more dramatic than for a woman today to throw her wedding ring away.

Therefore, Paul objected to those wives who appeared in public worship with hair hanging loose, uncovered before the eyes of the congregation. It was the same, he argued, as if they had their hair cut close (the style of prostitutes) or as if they had their heads shaved. To take such a liberty with her hair would shame a wife's "head," her husband. It was not a matter of a woman's hair being unseemly—Paul stated that it is her "glory." But she herself is the glory of her husband, and she should not shame him. The question is not what a woman does with her head, but what she says by what she does with her head.

Since customs have changed and hairstyles no longer mean what they did in the societies of Paul's time, his specific instructions are no longer relevant to modern Christians. However, the principle behind these instructions, of being sensitive to what message our dress codes and styles convey to others, still holds.

What of the Angels?

In the midst of this passage, Paul made a strong assertion that has puzzled many readers. He wrote, "Therefore the woman ought to have authority on the head, because of the angels" (1 Cor. 11:10). Some translators assume that Paul was speaking metaphorically when he wrote of authority for women, and so they word this sentence, "Therefore, a woman ought to wear a veil, because of the angels." What would wearing a veil have to do with angels? Tertullian offered one suggestion. He believed that if angels looked down and saw women without veils, they might fall in love with them!

The word Paul used, however, is not the word for veil. It is *exousia* (ex-OU-see-ah), a word used of kings and magistrates. It was used by Christ when he said that he had the authority to forgive sins (Matt. 9:6) and that he was given all authority in heaven and on earth (Matt. 28:18). It is used many times in the New Testament, and it means just what the English equivalent says—"power," "right," "strength," "authority." It is never used metaphorically to stand for a piece of clothing.

To explain with certainty the phrase "on the head" is impossible. The "therefore" at the beginning of the sentence refers back to Paul's phrase "woman is the glory of man"—"therefore" a woman ought to have authority "on the head." Does "head" designate her own physical head or does it mean her husband? The use of *epi* with *exousia* strongly suggests the latter, because elsewhere *exousia epi* means "authority over" someone or something (for example, in Matt. 9:6 and 28:18 those words are used in the phrase "authority on earth," and in Luke 9:1 they are used in the phrase "authority over demons").

If this is what Paul meant, he did not elaborate on how much or what kind of authority a woman is to exercise over her husband. One thing is certain, however: Paul affirmed that women are given authority in the Church.

Then what do angels have to do with authority? Before Pentecost, women were not recognized as spiritually equal with men. But on that day, Peter proclaimed that Joel's words had now come true, that both sons and daughters would prophesy and both men slaves and women slaves would receive the Holy Spirit. Women as well as men would receive communication from God.

This spiritual authority now given to women as well as men was foreshadowed in the Gospels by the action of angels. An angel came to Mary to enlist her cooperation in the birth of the Christ child. And two angels announced the resurrection of Jesus to Mary Magdalene, Joanna, and Mary the mother of James at the empty tomb (Luke 24:1–12).[6] The fact that angels came to women affirms the spiritual authority women may enjoy from God and that they may exercise within the church of Christ.

Perhaps this is what Paul had in mind when he said that a woman should have authority on the head "because of the angels." But this interpretation is by no means certain. It may be that the thought Paul had was known only to him and the recipients of his letter, and is now lost.

Paul's Message About Women's Attire

In one of Paul's letters to his beloved Timothy, he added an appeal regarding women's attire (1 Tim. 2:8–10). He began by stating a desire that men should lift up "holy hands without wrath and doubting." The word translated "doubting" is *dialogismos* (dee-ah-lo-gis-MOS). It can mean either "doubting" or "quarreling." In the context, it would seem likely that Paul meant to say doubting, but since the word is associated with one meaning "wrath," it could just as well mean "quarreling." Perhaps Paul meant both.

Then Paul turned to another matter that, like quarreling, can divide people within the Church: the matter of how women dress. "In like manner also," the Authorized (King James) Version reads, "that women adorn themselves in modest apparel, with shamefacedness and sobriety; not with braided hair, or gold, or pearls, or costly array; but (which becometh women professing godliness) with good works." More modern translations replace the word *shamefacedness* with its modern equivalent, *modesty*. The Greek word *aidous* (aye-DOUS) also means "reverence" and "respect." Its partner word, *sophrosune* (so-fro-SOON-ay), translated "sobriety," is not a word referring to alcoholic drinks. Instead, it describes someone who has good judgment, self-control, who can act with moderation.

Paul asked that the clothing women choose be modest (the Revised Standard Version reads "seemly"). Once Jesus described a man who drove out demons from his house. Later the demons returned and found the house empty, swept clean, and put in order (Matt. 12:44; Luke 11:25). The word for "put in order" is *kosmeo* (kos-ME-o). When Paul asked women to choose modest clothing, he used a form of this word. It means "put in order," "adorn," "make beautiful or attractive." In other words, Paul admonished Christian women to choose clothing that is orderly and attractive, but to do so with a sense of good judgment and moderation.

Paul then added a note about jewelry. Unfortunately, most translations overlook one word, and leave the impression that Paul was forbidding women from wearing any kind of jewelry or braiding their hair. The literal translation reads, "not with braiding and gold, or pearls or costly outer clothing."

Paul mentioned pearls because they were the most expensive gems of the ancient world (compare Jesus' parable of the pearl of great price, so costly that a man had to sell all he owned in order to buy it [Matt. 13:45-46]). Modern cultured pearls have brought this item of beauty to within modest prices. But even before mentioning costly pearls, Paul wrote of "braiding and gold." Here he used the word *kai* (and), braiding *and* gold. Then he wrote "or" pearls, "or" costly outer clothing. Paul was not forbidding the wearing of gold nor the braiding of hair per se, but the practice of braiding gold items into one's hair.

In the time of Paul, the Greek *hetairai* were schooled by older prostitutes in the fine art of cosmetics, fashion, and adornment.

One of their practices involved braiding pieces of gold jewelry into their hair, an artistic touch that more wealthy matrons began to imitate. It may seem strange that respectable women would follow the styles of courtesans, but in Rome, where prostitutes were required by law to make their hair yellow, it became a fad among married women to peroxide their hair or else to wear blond wigs!

Paul warned women in the Church not to adorn themselves in the style of courtesans. Or to wear extremely expensive pearls.

Last, Paul urged women to avoid costly "array," a word that in Greek refers to outer garments (a cloak or robe or stole). The arrangement of the wording places the emphasis on "costly," indicating that Paul was not denying women the right to wear warm clothing, but urging them to choose garments that are modest in cost.

A woman who manages a jewelry store once related to me how another woman wearing an expensive fur coat entered the store and informed the salesperson that true Christians do not wear gold jewelry because it is forbidden by Scripture. The woman misunderstood Paul's admonition to women: wear clothing that is tasteful and attractive, not disheveled or ostentatious, and avoid jewelry that is extravagant in cost or worn in the style associated with courtesans. Rather, women are to adorn themselves in ways suitable to one who professes the faith, remembering that the most beautiful aspect of a woman's appearance is not her attire but her good works in Christian love.

Questions for Thought and Discussion

1. Paul spent some time writing about hair styles, head coverings, cost of clothing, and symbolism of jewelry. Are these matters really that important? Why or why not?
2. In this chapter the statement is made, "since customs have changed and hair styles no longer mean what they did in

the societies of Paul's time, his specific instructions are no longer relevant to modern Christians." Do you agree or disagree? Why?

3. Many women in Muslim countries even today prefer to wear veils across their faces whenever they go out in public places. Why do you think they find this custom comfortable?

4. This chapter states that Paul based his instructions about head wear on the belief that "what one does with one's head . . . makes a theological statement." Is it true today that what we wear during worship makes a statement about our religious beliefs? If so, what statements are being made in our churches? Should clothing be given such theological importance in the church? Why or why not?

5. Paul's words indicate that what a wife may do with her hair will reflect on her husband. In what ways would this be true today for wives?

6. Paul states that women are to have authority, and he does so at the conclusion of his discourse on hair styles and head wear. How are hair and dress styles today associated with the matter of authority?

6. Is Celibacy Holy?

Soon after the age of the apostles, a notion arose within the Church that true holiness and piety is achieved by a believer only if that person withdraws from entangling relationships with others and lives a life of solitude and denial. After all, did not Jesus warn that "the one who loves father and mother more than me is not worthy of me, and the one loving son or daughter more than me is not worthy of me" (Matt. 10:37)? And did not Jesus call us to leave behind our worldly attachments and family bonds, saying, "And everyone who left houses or brothers or sisters or father or mother or children or fields for my name's sake will receive manifold and will inherit eternal life" (Matt. 19:29)? Therefore it was believed that the true believer will disengage himself or herself from property and kin alike in the pursuit of true spiritual wealth.

And while Jesus did not mention leaving one's marriage partner for his sake, he did speak of those who have made themselves eunuchs for the kingdom of God (Matt. 19:12), perhaps alluding to his own forsaking of marriage in order to fulfill his ministry. Although Jesus elsewhere defended marriage as a gift of God that is not to be violated (Matt. 19:3–9), nonetheless the words of Paul in 1 Corinthians 7 were used in subsequent centuries to defend the practice of refusing the divine gift of marriage in order to better pursue higher divine gifts. Celibacy became a means, if not a mark, of holiness.

Did Paul, in fact, promote celibacy among Christians? A quick reading of that passage would lead one to conclude that Paul ranked single Christians above married ones and regarded sexual intimacy in marriage as a compromise with our human desires—desires that, if unchecked, would lead us to burn in hell. Is this what Paul really meant?

The Jewish Way of Marriage

In the days of Paul, marriage was regarded as mandatory among Jews. Rabbi Eleazer taught that "a man who has no wife is not even a man."[1] His reasoning was that God created male and female and called them "man" (Gen. 5:2); therefore, a man is not a man unless he is married.

Indeed, many believed that marriages were arranged by God. This notion originated in the delightful story of the marriage of Isaac to Rebekah (Genesis 24). Abraham was a widower, living in the land of Canaan, and he was concerned that his son Isaac should find a proper wife, a woman not from among the Canaanites but from Abraham's kin back in Mesopotamia. So Abraham decided to take matters into his own hand's (after all, Isaac was a mere forty years old at that time). Abraham solemnly commissioned his oldest servant to travel back to his country of origin and there select a fine wife for his son Isaac from among Abraham's kindred.

The servant made the long journey, arriving at the city of Nahor. He decided that one meets more maidens at the city well than anywhere else, so he placed himself at that location. Then he prayed to God for a sign. "Grant me success today," he pleaded, informing the Almighty that he was now standing by a spring of water, watching the daughters of the men of the city coming to draw water. "Now," he continued, "let it be that when I ask a maiden for a drink of water, she should offer me a drink and—more than that—should offer to provide water for my camels as well; and let it be that maiden is the one whom you have appointed for your servant Isaac."

Even before he had finished this prayer, Rebekah arrived and descended to the spring with a water jar upon her shoulder. The servant of Abraham watched her, noting her beauty and that she was a virgin (how he knew this, the reader is not informed). When she ascended with a jar full of water, the servant ran to her and asked for a drink. She quickly honored his request and generously offered to bear water for his camels as well. The servant stared at her in silence, wondering whether this was an answer to his prayer.

Assuming the best, he offered her a nose-ring and several bracelets, all of gold. She took these to her father Bethuel and her brother Laban, who then showered the servant with offers of hospitality. When the servant had explained his mission and how the sign he had asked for from God had been granted in the thoughtful actions of Rebekah, both Laban and Bethuel responded by exclaiming, "The thing comes from the Lord" (Gen. 24:50). Later generations of Jews regarded this statement as proof that all marriages are made in heaven.

One proverb reads, "House and wealth are inherited from fathers, but a prudent wife is from the Lord" (Prov. 19:14), and rabbis taught that God sits in heaven arranging marriages. In the charming story of Tobit, the angel assures this young man that his kinswoman Sarah "was destined for you from eternity" (Tob. 6:17), and rabbis taught that forty days before the child is formed a heavenly voice proclaims its mate.

In spite of these romantic ideas, marriage was seen primarily as a means of providing children. The commandment that God gave to Adam and Eve, "Be fruitful and multiply" (Gen. 1:28), taught the rabbis, applies to all, and to fail in the duty of procreation was considered the same as murder.[2] It is to diminish the divine image, for "God made man in His image" (Gen. 9:6), argued Rabbi Akiba.[3] Another rabbi referred to the Shekhinah, the divine glory of God, and asked, "If you have no descendants, upon whom will the Shekhinah rest? Upon trees and stones?"[4]

The yearning of Abraham for a son and God's promise to him of descendants became a major theme in the Jewish view of marriage. All men were expected to father children (a term that according to the school of Shammai means two sons and according to the school of Hillel means a son and a daughter). If a couple were childless after ten years of marriage, the husband was instructed to divorce his wife and marry another in order to fulfill the commandment to be fruitful and multiply.[5] Only in time of great national disaster was marriage and bearing children discouraged.[6]

The Economics of Sexual Purity

At first glance, the Old Testament laws, in their severity, seem to place a strong moral wall of protection against sexual misconduct. Both rape and adultery (as well as a number of other sexual crimes) were punishable by death, and virginity at the time of marriage was so highly prized that a bride who could not demonstrate hymenal bleeding on her wedding night could be stoned to death for entering into marriage unchaste (Deut. 22:13–21).

These laws, however, were based not on moral but on economic principles. A young woman belonged to her father until the time of her marriage, when she became the property of her husband. (A father, for example, could sell his daughter to a man as a concubine (Exod. 21:7).) And since a virgin was much more valuable in the marriage market, the loss of her virginity was regarded as property damage to her father or merchandise damage to her groom. Therefore, for example, if a man seduced a virgin who was not betrothed (that is, not under contract to marry a certain man), he was required to pay the woman's father the amount that the father would have received at the time of her wedding were she still a virgin (Exod. 22:16–17). Or, if a man raped a virgin who was not betrothed, he was required to pay the father in the same way for the loss of value, and to marry the woman as well (Deut. 22:28–29). And if a man raped a woman who was betrothed to another man, he was stoned to death for his crime, not because he had violated the woman, but because he had violated his neighbor's wife (Deut. 22:23–27).

Within marriage, the wife was regarded as her husband's property, and if she allowed any other man to have sexual intercourse with her, she was put to death (Gen. 38:24; Ezek. 16:38–40, 23:45–47; John 8:5). A man, however, while forbidden from commiting adultery with his neighbor's wife, might marry as many women as he wished or have as many concubines as he wished. Moreover, he might divorce his wife and marry another, while his wife was provided no legal means to obtain a divorce except in extremely rare instances.

At the time of Paul, this double standard was clearly evident. The Mishnah, for example, has much to say about the woman who is suspected of committing adultery, but says nothing about the man who might be unfaithful to his wife. The Gospel of John tells of an incident in which the Pharisees advocated killing a woman found committing adultery, but no mention is made of the man involved with her in this crime—as if she had somehow committed adultery all by herself (John 8:3–11).

Although the Jewish rabbis equated adultery with idolatry and murder, the number of men who divorced their wives in order to marry others was so great that many Jewish girls were refusing to marry. The law read, "When a man has taken a wife and married her, if then she finds no favor in his eyes because he has found some uncleanness in her, and he writes her a bill of divorce and puts it in her hand and sends her out of his house" (Deut. 24:1). The interpretation of this scripture focused on the meaning of "some uncleanness" as a legal grounds for divorce. The school of Shammai defined it as meaning unfaithfulness and only unfaithfulness. There could be no cause for divorce except adultery. "Let the wife be as mischievous as the wife of Ahab," the saying went, "she cannot be divorced except for adultery." The school of Hillel, however, was much more lenient in interpreting this law. Hillel and his followers defined "some uncleanness" to mean anything she did that displeased her husband—speaking disrepectfully of his parents, for example, or spoiling his dinner with too much salt, or yelling at him. Rabbi Akiba even interpreted the phrase to mean that a man might divorce his wife if he found another woman who was more attractive than her!

Moreover, within marriage a man might impose a monetary fine upon his wife's dowry if she refused sexual intercourse with him, even to the point of depleting the dowry entirely and holding her in debt against any inheritance she might someday receive.[7] On the other hand, the husband might vow to refrain from sexual intercourse against his wife's will for up to a month at a time, depending upon his purpose and occupation.[8]

Marriage Among the Gentiles

While Aristotle argued at one point against the view that marriage had the primary function of procreation,[9] elsewhere he defended the view that marriage is above all else a means of bearing and raising children,[10] echoed later in Demosthenes' famous dictum, "we have. . .wives to bring up legitimate children and to be faithful stewards in household matters." The Greek husband demanded that his wife be faithful to him, and she was secluded in the home without any social outlet. She was not even allowed to have meals with the men of the household. But for men, using prostitutes as sexual outlets was the norm, carrying no stigma or discredit whatsoever. Adultery was regarded as a crime of property against the husband, while prostitution was the normal means of keeping the sexual drives of Greek and Roman men under control.[11]

Few means of livelihood were available to an unmarried woman other than prostitution. In Rome, prostitution was not held in as high esteem as in Greek society, but nonetheless it remained as a social institution (which, of course, was taxed by the government!). Cicero (106–43 B.C.), in his speech, "In Defense of Caelius," observed, "But if there be any one who thinks that youth is to be wholly interdicted from amours with courtesans, he certainly is very strict indeed. I cannot deny what he says; but still he is at variance not only with the licence of the present age, but even with the habits of our ancestors, and with what they used to consider allowable. For when was the time that men were not used to act in this manner? when was such conduct found fault with? when was it not permitted? when, in short, was the time when that which is lawful was not lawful?"[12]

Marriages among Roman couples were usually arranged by the girl's father, and marriage was regarded as a matter of duty rather than of love. Girls were married soon after puberty (sometimes as young as ten years of age). About one-fourth of them were married before reaching the age of fourteen, and after the age of nineteen any unmarried ones were regarded as spinsters. Men were often much older at the time of marriage. (For example, Augustine's widowed mother arranged for him to be married to a girl of ten when he was thirty-one years old. However, he refused the match.)

Traditionally, Roman husbands expected their wives to be faithful; they, however, held no such standards for themselves. Adultery was considered wrong, because it violated another man's property. For example, Cato "the Censor" (234–149 B.C.), a Roman statesman who endeavored to restore the moral standards of the early days of the republic, recalled how "if you were to take your wife in adultery, you could kill her with impunity, without any court judgment; but if you were involved in adultery, she would not dare to lift a finger against you, for it is unlawful."[13] Given such a double standard, Cato was surprised that his son and daughter-in-law objected to his sexual intimacy with a slave while his wife was still alive.

Indeed, most of the emperors had mistresses or concubines. The Emperor Constantine, the first Roman ruler to espouse Christianity, was himself the son of his father's concubine, Helena, the woman who built the Church of the Holy Sepulchre in Jerusalem. When the wife of Aurelius Verus (A.D. 130–169)—who shared imperial power with Marcus Aurelius—accused him of associating with other women, he replied that she must remember that the title of wife was one of dignity, not of pleasure.

In the first five hundred years of the Roman state, not a single divorce was recorded, not until the year 234 B.C. when a certain Spurius Carvilius Ruga divorced his wife because she was barren and he wanted a child. But by the time of Paul, divorce among Romans was as common as marriage.

Greek thought and culture (including the deprecation of women and marriage) had begun to permeate Roman society by the second century before Christ. The double standard gave way to no standard at all. And the resulting sexual chaos was, of course, blamed on women. In 18 B.C., Caesar Augustus introduced laws to stem the tide of higher and higher divorce rates, resulting in lower and lower birth rates and a dwindling population. These laws sought to punish guilty wives and their lovers with exile from Rome and confiscation of their property. Judging by the writings from that period of Roman history, Augustus's attempts proved to be futile. "Sooner will the seas be dried up," declared Sextus Propertius (c. 50–15 B.C.), a poet and friend of Ovid's, "than our women reformed."[14] His words were prophetic, if chauvinistic.

"He is a countrified lout, who objects when his wife does some cheating,"quipped Ovid in "The Loves," "yes, and an ignorant lout, blind to the ways of our town. . . ." He asks his fellow Roman males, "Why take a beautiful wife, if all you want is a pure one? Every natural law says you can't have it both ways."[15] The Stoic philosopher Seneca (c. 54 B.C.–A.D. 39) described women who married to be divorced and divorced to be married, adding that "only the ugly are loyal." He observed that women get husbands only as decoys for lovers, and the woman "who is content to have only two followers is a paragon of virtue."[16] Tacitus, a contemporary of Paul's, recorded that seduction was the spirit of the age.

About one woman, Juvenal (c. A.D. 60-140) wrote, "will Hiberina think one man enough? You'd find it much less trouble to make her agree to being blinded in one eye."[17] He mentioned another woman who had had eight husbands in five years. Martial, a friend of Juvenal's, spoke of one who had ten husbands. And another man declared in a speech, "If we could do without wives, we would be rid of that nuisance. But since nature has decreed that we can neither live comfortably with them, nor live at all without them, we must look rather to our permanent interests than to passing pleasure."[18] Even though such words sound as if they were spoken tongue-in-cheek, Caesar Augustus later quoted them in earnest agreement.

A saying developed among Roman men that "marriage brings only two happy days—the day when the husband first clasps his wife to his breast, and the day when he lays her in the tomb." The historian William Lecky described the change in Roman society as "that outburst of ungovernable and almost frantic depravity which followed upon the contact with Greece."[19]

The Stoic Disdain of Sexual Pleasure

Greek sexual extravagence led to a reaction among the followers of Zeno's philosophy of Stoicism. As mentioned in chapter 1, this philosophy warned men that love for a woman and sexual interests distract a man from the higher pursuit of wisdom. Women, therefore, were seen as hindrances to intellectual and spiritual growth—a view not unlike that held by Christian hermits, forerunners of the monastic movement in church history.

In the Roman period, Stoicism continued to paint all sexuality as dangerous. Musonius Rufus, a first-century A.D. Stoic teacher, argued that sexual intercourse should be allowed only for preservation of the race and never for pleasure, even within marriage.[20] Seneca agreed, stating, "A wise man ought to love his wife with judgment, not affection. Let him control his impulse and not be borne headlong into copulation. Nothing is fouler than to love a wife like an adulteress. Certainly those who say that they united themselves to wives to produce children for the sake of the state and the human race ought, at any rate, to imitate the beasts, and when their wife's belly swells not destroy the offspring. Let them show themselves to their wives not as lovers, but as husbands."[21]

Aulus Celsus, who compiled an encyclopedia in the first century A.D., wrote that sexual "intercourse neither should be avidly desired, nor should it be feared very much. Rarely performed, it revives the bodies, performed frequently it weakens. However, since nature, and not number, should be considered in frequency with consideration of age and the body, sexual union is recognized as not harmful when it is followed by neither apathy nor pain."[22] Early in the next century, Soranus of Ephesus, one of the most noted Greek physicians in Rome at that time, taught that sexual intercourse was harmful and that "permanent virginity" was desirable.[23] A contemporary of Soranus's, Philo, a Jew in Alexandria who sought to combine the writings of Moses with Greek philosophy, argued that sex for pleasure was "like pigs or goats in quest of enjoyment."[24] By the third century A.D., Stoic condemnation of sexual pleasure had reached its pinnacle with Porphyry (c. A.D. 232–304), who condemned sexual intercourse under any conditions as sinful.[25]

Paul's Answer to Sexual Chaos

Paul's goal of unifying Jews and Gentiles in the church of Jesus Christ compelled him to address the issues of sexual mores and marriage customs among both cultures. He was aware of the Jewish emphasis on sexual purity among women and the pressure upon single people to marry; he was also aware of the abuse by Jewish men of the laxity of divorce laws, so strongly condemned by Jesus in his teaching that divorce for any reason other than adultery was wrong (Matt. 5:31–32, 19:9; Mark 10:11–12[26]; Luke 16:18). Paul was cognizant of the ambivalent attitudes among Gentiles regarding sexual intercourse, ranging from the acceptance of prostitution as a normal social institution to the celibacy of some Stoics; he was also cognizant of the attitude, shared by both cultures, that wives are the possession and property of their husbands.

Paul's longest treatment of these issues is found in 1 Cor. 7:1–17, 25–40. He carefully distinguished between those teachings that came from the Lord and those that were his own opinions and advice. Here is a literal translation, with key words in Greek enclosed in parentheses, indicating that their meanings lose something in translation:

[1] Now, about the things of which you wrote: it is good for a man not to touch a woman, [2] but because of the immoralities (*porneia*) let each man have his own wife and each woman her own husband. [3] Let the husband pay the debt (*opheile*) to the wife, and likewise also the wife to the husband. [4] The wife has no authority of her own body, but the husband; and likewise also the husband has no authority of his own body, but the wife. [5] Do not deprive (*apostereo*) each other, unless by agreement for a time in order that you may have leisure for prayer and you may be together again, lest Satan put you to the test because of your lack of self-control. [6] Now, this I say by allowance, not by command. [7] I wish all persons to be as even myself; but each one has one's own gift of God, one thus, another thus.

[8] Now, I say to the unmarried and to the widows: it is good if they remain as I also; [9] but, if they do not exercise self-control, let them marry—it is better to marry than to be on fire.

[10] But to the ones who have married, I enjoin—not I, but the Lord—let not a woman be separated from her husband, [11] but if she is separated, let her remain unmarried or be reconciled to her husband. And let not a husband leave his wife.

[12] And to the rest say I—not the Lord—if any brother has an unbelieving wife, and this one consents to dwell with him, let him not leave her; [13] and a woman who has an unbelieving husband, and this one consents to dwell with her, let her not leave her husband. [14] For the unbelieving husband has been sanctified by the wife, and the unbelieving wife has been sanctified by the husband; since then your children are unclean, but now they are holy. [15] But, if the unbelieving one separates him/herself, let him/her be separated; the brother or sister has not been enslaved in such matters, but God has called you in peace. [16] Wife, do you know whether you will save your husband? Or husband, do you know whether you will save your wife? [17] Only, as the Lord has divided to each, as God has called each, so let one walk. And so I command in all the churches. . . .

[25] Now, about the virgins I do not have a command of the Lord, but I give an opinion, as having had mercy by the Lord to be faithful.

[26] I suppose therefore this to be good, because of the present necessity (*anagke*), that it is good for a man so to be. [27] Have you been bound [betrothed, promised in marriage] to a woman? Do not seek release. Have you been released from a woman? Do not seek a wife. [28] But if indeed you marry, you do not sin; and if the virgin marries, she does not sin. But such will have affliction in the flesh [in daily life], and I am sparing you that. [29] But this I say, brothers, the time has been shortened; for the rest, in order both the ones having wives may be as not having, [30] and the ones weeping as not weeping and the ones rejoicing as not rejoicing, and the ones buying as not holding, [31] and the ones using the world as not abusing—for the nature of this world is passing away. [32] But I wish you to be without care. The unmarried cares for the things of the Lord, how he may please the Lord; [33] but the married one cares for the things of the world, how he may please his wife [34]—and he has been divided. And the unmarried woman and the virgin cares for the things of the Lord, in order that she may be holy both in body and in the spirit; but the married one cares for the things of the world, how she may please her husband. [35] And I say this for your advantage, not in order that I may put a restraint on you, but for the lovely thing and for waiting on the Lord undistractedly. [36] But if anyone thinks to behave dishonorably toward his betrothed, if one is of strong passion—and so ought to be—as one wishes let one do; one does not sin, let them marry. [37] But one who stands firm in his heart, not having necessity (*anagke*) but has authority concerning his own will, and has decided in his own heart to keep his betrothed, he will do well. [38] Thus both the one marrying his betrothed does well and the one not marrying will do better.

[39] A wife has been bound to her husband for as long a time as he lives; but if the husband sleeps, she is free to be married to whom she wishes, only in the Lord. [40] But she is happier if she so remains, according to my opinion—and I think I also have the Spirit of God.

Three words in the first four sentences invite closer attention, offering additional insight into Paul's thinking. The first is *porneia* (por-NAY-ah), from which we derive the first half of the English word *pornography*. Paul normally used *porneia* in the singular, meaning "immorality," "unchastity," or "fornication"

(1 Cor. 5:1; 2 Cor. 12:21; Gal. 5:19; Eph. 5:3; Col. 3:5). But in this passage, he used *porneia* in the plural.

Some translators render it "immoralities," but it may be that Paul had in mind specific sexual temptations, as it appears in the context of how a man is not "to touch a woman" and how, because of *porneias*, it is better for men and women to be married. *Porneias* is a form of the noun *porne* (por-NAY), "prostitute," and itself can mean "prostitution." It seems likely that Paul, in writing to the church in Corinth, the prostitution center of the ancient world, was warning the men that they faced a constant and powerful temptation from this source. Indeed, the sentences preceding this passage admonish men not to join themselves to prostitutes (1 Cor. 6:15–20). While the Greeks saw no wrong in patronizing a brothel, Paul forbade it and commanded marriage as a way of avoiding such immorality.

The second word is *orpheile* (o-fie-LAY). It describes an obligation or duty one owes to another, or a debt one has vowed to pay. Taken one way, Paul might have been deprecating sexual intimacy in marriage by calling it a duty one owes to the other. In the context, however, Paul was using this word to mean that a married person cannot simply decide to refrain from sexual intercourse without the consent of the other.

The third word is *apostereo* (a-pos-ter-EE-o). It means "deprive," "steal from," "rob," "defraud." Paul was saying that refusing to have sexual intercourse with one's mate is a form of robbery or fraud.

One other word deserves special attention. In verse 26, Paul wrotes of the "present necessity." The first word, translated "present," may also mean "coming" or "impending." Therefore, the reader cannot be certain whether Paul was writing of something happening then or yet to come. The word translated "necessity" is *anagke* (an-ANG-kay). It can mean that which is forced upon us, what we are compelled to do, either by government authority or by nature. It can also refer to distress brought by a calamity of some kind.

Jesus used this word to describe a future calamity, filled with *anagke* and wrath, with people falling by the sword and the survivors taken into captivity (Luke 21:22). Because Jesus used it in this context, some scholars conclude that Paul meant the same thing in this passage; in that sense, Paul was saying that the end of the age is near, so it is better not to be married because of the distress that will precede the climax of history. Indeed, in verses 29–31, Paul used the kind of language one associates with predictions of the end times.

However, Jesus also used *anagke* when saying that it is necessary that temptations come (Matt. 18:7). This meaning would fit well with the subject that Paul was addressing, avoiding falling into sexual temptations.

Elsewhere, however, Paul used *anagke* in two different ways. He spoke of our *anagke*, necessity, to obey earthly rulers (Rom. 13:5) and the necessity he felt to preach the gospel (1 Cor. 9:16). In these instances, *anagke* is a compulsion that comes from an authority (the government or Christ). This meaning would fit with Paul's belief that being married can hinder one's service to the Lord by dividing one's loyalty between Christ and wife or husband.

More frequently, however, Paul used *anagke* still another way, to describe the hardships he had endured for Christ under persecution by enemies of the gospel. Paul had suffered *anagke*, along with afflictions, calamities, beatings, imprisonments, insults, persecutions, and difficulties (2 Cor. 6:4, 12:10; 1 Thess. 3:7). It is most likely that *anagke* as Paul used it in this passage about marriage means this kind of distress. In that sense, he was telling unmarried people to remain that way; because of the present hardships that believers must endure, he was saying, it is better not to have the responsibilities and cares that marriage brings. It is better to be unmarried if one must face persecution (verse 26). However, if one has decided to be married and is not under this kind of hardship (*anagke*), Paul added, but is under his own authority, let him "keep his betrothed" (literally, "keep his virgin")—that is, remain under contract to marry her (verse 27).

Paul upheld the highest of Jewish moral principles regarding sexuality. He often reminded his readers that adultery is wrong, but he extended this truth to condemn the methods men employed to commit "legal adultery" as well. Though prostitution was an integral part of society in Corinth, Athens, and Rome, Paul wrote that a man is not to join himself to a prostitute (1 Cor. 6:15–16), for such an act is immoral (1 Cor. 6:18, 7:2). Though polygamy was legal, for the Christian "each man should have his own wife and each wife her own husband" (verse 2). In 1 Timothy, Paul insisted that a male bishop or deacon have only one wife (1 Tim. 3:2, 12, 5:9).[27]

Paul also instructed his readers against premarital sex (verses 8–9 and 36–38), saying that if they are "on fire" with passion, they should marry. And Paul reminded those Jews and Gentiles who used divorce as a legal means of switching mates of the teachings Jesus gave concerning remarriage (verses 10–11).

In Paul's opinion, it is better to be single than to be married, because of the present (or impending) hardships or distress that Christians must face (verse 26). Moreover, a single person can serve the Lord without divided loyalties (verses 32–35). Paul himself was single (verses 7–8) and considered that best (verse 38). And if a Christian is married to an unbeliever who wishes to separate, that is permissible, Paul added (again reminding his readers that this was his own opinion—verses 12–15).

Paul would tell the Jewish rabbis who insisted that marriage is mandatory for all men that it is better to be single. But he would also tell those Stoics who spurned marriage as evil that it is good to be married. While Paul was careful to state that this was not a command of Christ for Christians to marry (verse 6), he also pointed out that a believer may lead an unbelieving marriage partner to salvation (verses 12–16). But Paul reminded his readers of how marriage brings responsibilities (verses 28b, 32–35) and distracts one from undivided service to the Lord. Later on, however, Paul mentioned that all the other apostles besides himself were married (1 Cor. 9:5). In other writings, Paul denounced those who, like the Stoics, forbid marriage (1 Tim. 4:3) and those who marry simply out of lust (1 Thess. 4:4–5).

Paul refused to echo the notion that women are the property of their husbands. In verses 3–5, he eliminated any possibility of a double standard for sex within marriage. Sexual intimacy is right and good; no husband or wife has the right to refrain without both of them agreeing to abstain—and then only for a brief time and only for the purpose of prayer, lest temptation lead to immorality. A husband cannot engage in sexual intercourse as he wills and with whom he wills, because his body is under the authority of his wife; and the same is true for a wife, for her body is under the authority of her husband.[28]

Nowhere did Paul intimate that the purpose of marriage is procreation. He anticipated that children would be produced, but he did not support the classical Greek and Jewish rabbinical idea that bearing children is the aim of marriage.

Nor did Paul leave any room for the notion that sexual intercourse is harmful, demeaning, or evil. Just before this passage, Paul reminded the Corinthian church that it is God's design that in marriage "the two shall become one flesh," leaving no doubt that sexual, and not just spiritual, intimacy was intended (1 Cor. 6:16).[29]

Paul recommended choosing to remain single, but not because marriage is wrong. There was no thought in his writing that a single person is thereby more holy or spiritual than a married person. It is just that a married person has more anxiety and troubles, and his or her interests are divided (verses 26, 32–35).

The notion that a celibate person is thereby more spiritual came not from Paul but from the Greek philosophy of Stoicism. It is no more scriptural than are the other teachings of Zeno, no more Christian than the writings of Plato. Moreover, the notion that single adults are not as spiritual as married persons would be challenged by Paul, as well as by the example of Jesus himself. Perhaps the final word regarding celibacy versus marriage in the Church is Paul's own conclusion on the matter, that each one has one's "own special gift from God, one of one kind and one of another" (1 Cor. 7:7).

Paul's plea for sexual purity and equality whether one is single or married, embodies the one idea of Christianity that was absolutely new to the ancient world. No other religion nor any philosophy had affirmed sexuality as a gift of God that must be exercised within specific moral boundaries, and no other religion nor any philosophy had so outspokenly declared the equality of men and women before God.

Questions for Thought and Discussion

1. In what ways does being single facilitate serving the Lord?
2. In what ways does being married increase one's ability to serve the Lord?
3. In the teaching of the Stoics, celibacy was commended and marriage was discouraged. How does this compare with the popular views of our own society? With the teachings of the churches today?
4. Is the double standard still with us in our society today? If so, why does it continue to survive so long?
5. There is a doctrine of the perpetual virginity of Mary, the mother of Jesus, which teaches that Mary remained a virgin all of her life. Defense of this teaching must include an explanation of the relationship of Jesus with those whom the New Testament refers to as his "brothers" (Matt. 13:55; Mark 6:2-3, Acts 1:13-14, Gal. 1:18-19) and an interpretation of the implication in Matthew 1:25 that Mary remained a virgin only until after the birth of Jesus. Regardless of whether or not Mary remained a virgin all of her life, the belief that she did so has remained very important to some Christians. Why might this be so?

6. In biblical times, virginity up to the time of marriage and fidelity during marriage on the part of women was of economic importance. Is sexual behavior in our society today effected by economics? If so, how?

7. The Slandered Apostle

Paul attempted to bring into one family of God both Gentiles and Jews, in spite of the fact that the customs and ideals of these two groups of people were often in conflict. Not satisfied with this one goal alone for the Church, Paul also sought to establish a sense of equality within the membership that was found nowhere else in the ancient world, so that masters and slaves and males and females would all be one in Christ Jesus.

Others, such as Philo, had attempted to combine Greek philosophy with Jewish Scripture, and still others had objected to the widespread practice of slavery or to various extreme abuses suffered by slaves. But the deprecation of women was at least as old as the philosophy of Athens, and any attempt to put into practice Paul's teaching that "there is neither male nor female, for you are all one in Christ Jesus" would meet deep and ages-strong resistance.

The ideal itself was an easy prey to criticism and fantasizing by a skeptical society in which women and religion were associated with orgiastic rites. Only if the Church lived within the boundaries of the strictest sexual morality could it maintain a sense of sexual equality among its members and stand up to the criticisms leveled at it by its neighbors.

Paul's Ideal versus Embedded Attitudes

Paul's instructions concerning women and marriage were in constant conflict with the teachings of Greek philosophers and Jewish rabbis. A battle was waged for centuries within the community of faith, pitting Paul's ideal against the ageless Hellenic and Jewish attitudes about the female sex.

A female is a deformed male, Aristotle taught.[1] Male and female are one in Christ, Paul declared (Gal. 3:28).

Women as well as men are to lead in worship, Paul noted (1 Cor. 11:4). Men and women are to be separate during worship, Jewish custom dictated, and only men count in determining a quorum (*minyan*) for worship.

Women are to learn, Paul insisted (1 Tim. 2:11). Women are inferior to men in their ability to reason, Aristotle argued.[2]

Sexual intercourse is harmful, many Stoics believed, and marriage distracts a man from the study of philosophy. Marriage and sexual intimacy are a gift from God, Paul observed (1 Cor. 11:12; Eph. 5:31; compare Gen. 1:27, 2:22–25).

However, in such a time as this, it is better for a believer who is unmarried to remain single, taught Paul (1 Cor. 7:7, 25–35, 39–40). A man who is not married is not even a man, declared the Jewish *Mishnah*.[3]

A man's courage is in commanding, a woman's in obeying, asserted Aristotle.[4] Husbands and wives are to be responsive to the needs of each other, Paul instructed (1 Cor. 7:3–5; Eph. 5:22–33).

Sexual intimacy must be confined to marriage, Paul insisted (1 Cor. 6:15–20, 7:1–2, 36–38; et al.). Prostitution is an ancient and hallowed institution, the Greeks responded.

Ever since Eve, the Jews were taught, women have been morally weak and a source of temptation to men. "Woman is the glory of man," Paul stated (1 Cor. 11:7).

A husband and wife are each to have authority over the body of the other, and they are not to refrain from sexual intimacy except for a brief time and then only when both agree, Paul instructed (1 Cor. 7:3–5). A man may abstain against his wife's wishes, the Jewish Mishnah read, but a man may impose a monetary fine against his wife if she refuses him.[5]

The authority over a woman belongs first to her father and then, when she is married, to her husband, Greek and Jewish laws agreed. A woman shall have authority on her own head, Paul insisted (1 Cor. 11:10).

Married couples shall remain so, Paul urged (1 Cor. 7:10–23). Not if the woman fails to bear sons, the Jewish rabbis declared.

During the second century A.D., one of Paul's great visions for the Church was lost. Fewer and fewer Jews accepted the Christian faith, and there developed an expanding rift between the two religions. But Paul's hope for the equality of the sexes within the Church met with continued success—for a time, at least. Even Tertullian, who wrote with ambivalence regarding the nature of woman, observed of men and women in the Church that they "perform their fasts, mutually teaching, mutually exhorting, mutually sustaining. Equally are they both found in the church of God; equally in straits, in persecutions, in refreshments. Neither hides from the other; neither shuns the other; neither is troublesome to the other."[6]

Clement of Alexandria, a contemporary of Tertullian's and head of the Christian school in that city until driven out by persecution in A.D. 203, insisted that men and women alike may "philosophize,"[7] and he defended the sanctity of marriage and parenthood. "Who are the two or three gathering in the name of Christ, among whom the Lord is in their midst?" Clement asked. "Does he not mean man, wife, and child by the three, seeing woman is made to match man by God?"[8]

An anonymous writer testified to the sexual morality of Christians within their ideal of equality. "They marry and have children like everyone else—but they do not expose their children [that is, leave newborn babies that are unwanted to die from exposure to the elements]. They have meals in common, but not wives. They are in the flesh, but they do not live after the flesh. They continue on earth, but their citizenship is in heaven."[9]

The Demise of Sexual Equality

But at last the ideal of sexual equality within the Church was dealt a mortal blow: Christianity became fashionable.

In the middle of the fourth century, the Emperor Constantine gave his favor to the faith of Christians, and those who would court imperial favor began to join the Church. Since the bishops of the Church had access to the Emperor's ear, ecclesiastical power and wealth increased. Many who became members of the Christian church were not particularly interested in the way this faith might transform society—indeed, they may not have cared much at all about the teachings of the Christ.

As the Church became more and more transformed by the world, its life took on more of the characteristics of Hellenized Roman society. Devout persons began to leave both church and city in a private search for spiritual growth and holiness. These hermits by their own example led people to associate celibacy with true devotion to Christ—an association of ideas that affirmed the Stoic disdain for sexual intimacy and marriage.

Slowly the teachings of Greek philosophy interbred with Christian theology, producing a brood of beliefs that were often pagan in their assumptions. For example, many of the church leaders in the fourth century accepted without question the idea that marriage and sexual intimacy were detrimental to one's spirituality. Gregory of Nyssa (c. 331–396), one of the fathers of the Eastern church, imagined that if Adam and Eve had not sinned and had remained in a state of innocence, then the human race in Paradise would have been multiplied by some means other than copulation.[10]

Before his conversion, Augustine (354–430) wanted to believe in the Christian gospel; yet, on the other hand, he seemed unable to rid his life of its hectic and sordid habits. "Give me chastity and continency," he prayed, "only not yet." He seemed to see only two alternatives, to continue his lustful and directionless life, or else to give up "the world" for an ascetic, celibate life. Apparently he never considered the possibility of becoming a Christian teacher with a wife and family.[11]

In fact, both Augustine and Jerome wondered if a married person would be admitted into heaven. Augustine argued that God made man and woman in order to provide a means for the continuance of the human race, but Augustine imagined that if sin had not entered the world reproduction would have been accomplished "without ardent or wanton incentive, with calmness of soul and body."[12] In such a state of purity, intercourse would be accomplished "without prejudice to virginal integrity.[13]"

The writings of the church fathers—especially those of Augustine—deeply influenced the thinking of subsequent generations, to the point that these became authoritative for the Church, next to the Bible itself. And eventually the teachings of the philosopher Aristotle were accepted as almost infallible. These two giant sources of ideas—Augustine the Christian saint and Aristotle the pre-Christian philosopher—provided male church leaders with a sexual bias that naturally led them to interpret Paul's writings in a like manner of thought.

At last the conflict between Paul's demand for sexual equality within the Church and the deprecation of women in Greek philosophy was resolved: the ideas of Aristotle prevailed, bolstered by Augustine and other writers, and the words of Paul were reinterpreted and quoted in defense of practices that Paul opposed!

While this progressive victory of Greek attitudes over apostolic idealism was gradual—and perhaps unconscious—nonetheless Paul's own words were used as authority to prohibit that which he advocated. In that sense, Paul the apostle has been slandered and is still being slandered today.

Aquinas's Final Defeat of Paul's Ideal

The defeat of Paul's ideal of sexual equality culminated in the writings of Thomas Aquinas, who was canonized less than fifty years after his death. Aquinas was so revered in his own lifetime that after his death his flesh was boiled away from his bones and these were sold as holy relics![14] Pope Leo XIII in 1879 declared Saint Thomas Aquinas to be the one theologian whose writings must be studied in all Roman Catholic colleges, universities, and seminaries. His influence has not been limited to Roman Catholics, however; one Protestant church historian described Aquinas as "undoubtedly the most influential thinker in Christian history,"[15] and much of his teaching about women—and even some of Aquinas's own expressions—is still preached from numerous Protestant pulpits.

Aquinas wrote hymns, sermons, commentaries on Scripture, and, most important, an enormous summary of Christian theology that enabled earnest intellectuals of his day to reaffirm the Christian faith. Skeptics had used the teachings of Aristotle to refute the teachings of the Church, and Aquinas, as a brilliant and prodigious scholar, used the writings of Aristotle in defending Catholic beliefs. He demonstrated how the natural truths within Greek philosophy (that is, truths gained by observation and reason) affirm and are complemented by revealed truths within Christian theology (that is, truths gained by reading the Scriptures and the writings of the church fathers, especially those of Augustine).

Despite his skillful use of logic in questioning the conclusions of those who challenged Christian theology, however, Aquinas was all too quick to affirm the class system of medieval society, the paternalistic pattern of family life, and the authority of ecclesiastical leaders and nobility. Aquinas could not conceive of woman being equal to man, either before or after the fall of the first couple in Eden. He agreed with Aristotle that woman "is defective and misbegotten."[16]

Aristotle assumed (perhaps based on his conviction that maleness is to be equated with strength and superiority) that the male seed implanted in the female will produce male offspring as a matter of course, unless this seed is defective or else is affected negatively by "some external influence, such as that of a south wind which is moist."[17] Aquinas taught that while it is true that woman is misbegotten, it is God's intention that woman be included in humanity, in order that she may be Adam's helper. However, the only way that Eve could be a helper to Adam was in terms of "the work of generation," the female's ability to give birth to children; in any other capacity a man would be a better helper for Adam. After all, "man can be more efficiently helped by another man in other works," Aquinas observed.[18]

Paul's ideal that there is "neither male nor female, for you are all one in Christ Jesus" was limited in Aquinas's interpretation to "the social union of man and woman."[19] He referred to the creation of Eve from Adam's rib in defining this relationship: "For the woman should neither use authority over man, and so she was not made from his head; nor was it right for her to be subject to man's contempt as his slave, and so she was not made from his feet."[20] However, in Aquinas's views woman was subject to man from the beginning.

Aquinas, like Aristotle, differentiated between the kind of subjection a man might expect from his slave and the kind he might expect from his wife. One kind of subjection is "servile, by virtue of which a superior makes use of a subject for his own benefit." The other kind of subjection differs in that "the superior makes use of his subjects for their own benefit and good; and this kind of subjection existed even before sin."[21] It is this latter kind of subjection that applies to women, according to Aquinas, "because in man the discernment of reason predominates."[22] The understanding of subjection that Aquinas held was the same as the one that had been taught by Aristotle, not the one that had been commended by Jesus for all his disciples (Mark 10:42–45) nor the one that had been commended by Paul for all church members, including husbands and wives (Eph. 5:21).

For Aquinas, man is the thinker and woman is the childbearer, a view held in modern times by the minister who declared on radio that only men can preach and teach because "God made roosters to crow and hens to lay eggs."[23] Aquinas disregarded all of Paul's writings that would defend the notion that women and men are equal, and lifted out of context Paul's words about how woman is the glory of man and was created for man. Aquinas quoted and affirmed the statement in Genesis that God created both male and female in His image (Gen. 1:27), but then defined different degrees in which a person can be in the image of God. Both men and women, he argued, are in the image of God in possessing "a natural aptitude for understanding and loving God"; however, only the male "actually or habitually knows and loves God," not the female, "for man is the beginning and end of woman, just as God is the beginning and end of every creature."[24] Woman, therefore, can fulfill her divine destiny only in the matter of bearing children for man; "she was not fitted to help man except in generation, because another man would have proved a more effective help in anything else."[25]

However, according to Aquinas, sexual intercourse is sinful when it is a source of "vehement delight" for the man; it causes him to become more like the beasts than at any other moment in his life.[26] (Apparently Aquinas believed that the basest of human character emerges not in the heat of riots or wars or exploitation, but in the passion of sexual union of man and woman.) And while coitus would have been necessary for the production of the human race, Aquinas continued, and would have been necessary even if sin had not entered the world, nonetheless in the state of innocence it would have been accomplished, as Augustine said, "without concupiscence. All the bodily members would have been equally moved by the will, without ardent or wanton incentive, with calmness of soul and body."[27]

With Aquinas, the deprecation of womanhood was completely infused into Christian theology, based upon the authority of Aristotle and Augustine and Aquinas's interpretation of the words of the apostle Paul. Thus, those who have benefited from the superb scholarship of Thomas Aquinas—Protestants as well as Catholics —have also inherited his Grecian conviction of the inferiority of females to males. Even Saint Thomas More (1478–1535), the capable scholar and statesman who courageously opposed King Henry VIII's divorce from Catherine of Aragon, and who is remembered for his advocacy of education for women as well as men, nonetheless regarded women as intellectually secondary to men. "If it be true that the soil of woman's brain is poor," he wrote, "and more apt to bear bracken than corn— by so saying, many prevent women from study—I think, on the contrary, that a woman's mind is on that account all the more dilligently to be cultivated, that nature's defect may be redressed by industry."[28]

Paul's model for husbands and wives, based on the way that Christ is head of the Church by being its savior—even willing to die for his beloved—was lost to Christian theology. Instead, Aquinas by example established Aristotle's model, in which the husband is the lord of his wife, as more authoritative for Christians. Saint Robert Bellarmine (1542–1621), in a letter to his niece, offered a written example of how this interpretation of Scripture was unquestioningly taught to Christian couples:

. . . your husband should be regarded as lord and master, and you must know that he is to be obeyed and honoured as the head. Thus St. Peter tells us that Sarah, Abraham's wife, addressed him as lord, not husband. St. Augustine also, in speaking of his mother St. Monica, recounts how she would remain meek and silent, returning no answer when her husband burst in storming and raging; although she knew perfectly well he was furiously angry, she refused to quarrel with him, until finally her humility and modesty won him over for God. And indeed when her neighbours came to complain that their husbands beat them, she could reply that no doubt they deserved it, they were probably trying to usurp his position as head of the house. She added that they should look upon matrimony as a deed of sale in which they were sold into servitude; as slaves, they should be humble and submissive. Even though husbands ought to look upon their wives not as slaves but as partners, nevertheless the wife should always regard her husband as master.[29]

Surely in the long history of Christian teachings regarding the relationship of women and men, the model that gained favor in the Church was not the one voiced by Paul, but by a pagan philosopher five centuries older, defended in the sanctuaries and cathedrals of the Christian faith by quoting the words of Paul, as translated, out of context, without reference to that ideal close to Paul's heart that he so earnestly sought for the church, that there be sexual equality among Christians— "neither male nor female, for you are all one in Christ Jesus."

Questions for Thought and Discussion

1. Aquinas wrote of a kind of subjection in which "the superior makes use of his subjects for their own benefit and good." Is this kind of relationship realistic between government and citizens? Between clergy and laity? Between husband and wife?
2. In what ways do you see Aquinas's thinking still influencing religious teachings about women and about marriage?
3. In this chapter appears the statement, "only if the church lived within the boundaries of the strictest of sexual morality could it maintain a sense of sexual equality among its members. . . ." Is the issue of sexual equality today still effected by sexual mores and practices? If so, how? If not, why?
4. Paul taught that sexual intercourse should be confined to marriage. Is that a realistic expectation for Christians today? Why or why not?
5. How can the church maintain a standard of sexual morality and still be a community of grace in which those who do not live up to its moral standards nonetheless will find acceptance and worth?
6. In what ways, if any, should the lifestyle of church members differ from those of society in general? Why? What problems would any such differences create?

NOTES

Chapter 1: *Where the Idea That Women Are Inferior to Men Really Began*

1. Herbert J. Muller, *Freedom in the Ancient World* (New York: Harper & Row, 1961), 318–19.
2. The middle portion of this quotation reads "neither slave nor free."While the subject of slavery and early Christianity is beyond the scope of this book, some have argued that Paul was just being poetical in this passage; he writes that there is neither slave nor free, neither male nor female, but in actual practice he condoned slavery and sexual inequality. Therefore, a summary of the subject of slavery may have incidental bearing on Paul's teachings about women. Paul's favorite title for himself was "slave of Christ." (Some translators soften this to "servant" of Christ, but the word is the same, and in actual practice a servant was in an even more pitiable position in ancient society than a slave, because a slave had some security at least.) Paul taught a modification of the relationship between master and slave, based on Christian love and a sense that we are all slaves for Christ. He admonished Philemon to greet his slave no longer as a slave, but as a brother (Philem.1:15–16). Following Paul's teaching, the early Church recognized no status difference between master and slave. All persons were to be seated together. The word *slave*, although extremely common among graves of non-Christians, is never used in inscriptions in the Christian burials in the catacombs. Slaves were permitted to hold office within the Church, even that of bishop and pope. According to Ignatius, a second-century bishop, church funds were used to buy freedom for a number of slaves (*Apostolic Constitutions 4,9*). Some Christians even surrendered their own freedom to ransom others from slavery (*I Clement 55*). Marriage among slaves was protected, and non-Christians were urged to free their slaves or allow them to purchase their own freedom. Clement wrote, "Slaves are men like ourselves," and Lactantius added, "Slaves are not slaves to us; we deem them brothers after the spirit, in religion, fellow-servants." Ambrose argued that a slave might be superior to his master in character and Augustine believed that God does not approve of slavery (as opposed to Aristotle's view that slavery is natural). Would that the early Church took Paul's words about "neither male nor female" as seriously as it took his words about "neither slave nor free"!
3. Dr. Arthur Verral, *Euripides the Rationalist*, quotation from T.R. Glover, *The Conflict of Religions in The Early Roman Empire* (Boston: Beacon 1960), 163.
4. Homer, *Odyssey*, trans. *Ennis Rees (New York: Random House, 1960)*, 9.114–15.
5. Plato, *Timaeus*, trans. *H.D.P. Lee (Baltimore: Penguin, 1965)*, 42A–C, 90C, 91A.

6. Plato, *The Republic*, trans. W.H.D. Rouse (*New York*: Mentor, *1956*), *454B*.
7. Ibid., 456A.
8. Ibid., 457A–D.
9. Xenophon, "Within the Home", *The Greek Reader* trans. A.L. Wholl (New York: Doubleday, 1943), 625.
10. Quoted by William Barclay *The Daily Study Bible*, vol. 10, 201.
11. Stephen Jay Gould, *Hen's Teeth and Horse's Toes* (New York: Norton, 1984), 244.
12. Aristotle, *Politics*, trans. *Oxford University, The Basic Works of Aristotle*, Richard McKean, editor (*New York*: *Random House, 1941*), 1.1259B.
13. Ibid.
14. Ibid., 1.1254A, 1259B, 1260A.
15. Ibid., 1.1254B.
16. Demosthenes, *Adv. Neaeram*, 122. Quotation by Marcus Barth, *The Anchor Bible* (New York: Doubleday, 1979), vol. 34A, 655.
17. Xenophon, ibid.
18. Vern and Bonnie Bullough, *Prostitution* (New York: Crown, 1978), 41–42.
19. Quoted and retranslated by T. R. Glover, *The Conflict of Religions* 51.
20. Ibid.
21. Ibid.
22. Herodotus, *Histories*, trans. *Aubrey de Selincourt* (*Baltimore*: Penguin, *1954*), 2.35.
23. Ptahhotep, trans. John A. Wilson, *Ancient Near Eastern Texts Relating to The Old Testament*, James B. Pritchard, ed. (Princeton University Press, 1950), 412.
24. Barbara S. Lesko, *The Remarkable Women of Ancient Egypt* (Berkeley: B. C. Scribe Publications, 1978), 30–31.
25. Diodorus Siculus, 1,27,2, quotation by Lesko, *The Remarkable Women*, 25.
26. Leipoldt, *Die Frau in der antiken Welt und im Urchirstentum*, 3rd ed. (Leipzig: Koehler & Amelang, 1965), 49; quoted by Marcus Barth, the Anchor Bible (New York: Doubleday, 1960), vol. 34A, p. 658, ft. 208.
27. *P. Oxy.*, 1380,214–15.
28. Muller, *Freedom*, 234.
29. Plutarch, "Conjudal Precepts", from *Plutarch's Essays and Miscellanies*, vol. 2, A. H. Clough and William W. Goodwin, editors (New York: Colonial, 1905), 8,48,20,11,33,16.
30. *Sotah* 3:4. All quotations from the Mishnah are translated by Herbert Danby (London: Oxford University Press, 1933).
31. All biblical quotations are the author's own unless otherwise noted.
32. Exod. 18:4; Deut. 33:7,26,29; Pss. 20:2, 33:20, 70:5, 89:19, 115:9, 121:1–2, 124:8, 146:5; other references are Isa. 30:5; Ezek. 12:14; Dan. 11:34; and Hos. 13:9.
33. The wording in Exod. 20:17 is almost identical.
34. Mishnah, *Ketuboth* 4:6, 6:1.
35. Ibid., 1:8, 7:6.
36. Mishnah, *Aboth* 1:5.
37. Talmud, *'Erubin* 53b, Unless otherwise noted, all quotes from the Babylonian Talmud are translated under the editorship of I. Epstein (London: Soncino, 1974).

38. William Barclay, *Daily Study Bible*, 2nd ed. (Edinburgh: St. Andrew Press, 1958), vol. 2, 142–43.
39. Talmud *Tos Berakoth* 7:18; *Bab. Menahoth* 43b.
40. *Sotah* 3.4.
41. Sexual intercourse by a man with his female slave, even when the slave was betrothed to be married to another, was not regarded as adultery in the Mosaic law. See Lev. 19:20.
42. Anchor Bible translation.
43. *Sayings of the Jewish Fathers*, 2nd ed., (Cambridge: University Press, 1897), 137–40.
44. See Mishnah, *Aboth* 1:5.
45. *Shabbath* 33b.
46. Magen Broshi, "Beware the Wiles of the Wanton Woman," *Biblical Archaeology Review* (July/August, 1983): 56.
47. Philo, *The Special Laws*, 3.178. All quotations of Philo are translated by F. H. Colson (Cambridge: Harvard University Press, 1968).
48. Philo, *On the Creation*, 165–66. Philo makes an exception regarding the ability of a woman to have good judgment in the case of Julia Augusta, great-grandmother of Emperor Caligula, for she "adorned the temple with golden vials and libation bowls and a multitude of other sumptuous offerings" and therein excelled other women, even though "the judgments of women as a rule are weaker and do not apprehend any mental conception apart from what their senses perceive" (*Gaius*, 319–20).
49. Philo, *Allegorical Interpretation of Genesis*, 2.49.
50. Philo, *Special Laws*, 3.169 (Compare 170–71 as well as *Flaccus*, 89).
51. Philo, *Hypothetica*, trans. 380.
52. Josephus, *Against Apion*, 2.25. All quotations of Josephus are translated by William Whiston (Cincinnati: Morgan, 1849),
53. Josephus, *Antiquities of the Jews*, 4.815.
54. Talmud, *Sannedrin*, trans. Lewis Browne, *The Wisdom of Israel* (New York: Random House, 1945), 211-12.
55. Tertullian, "On The Apparel of Women, trans. S. Thelwall, *Ante-Nicene Fathers* (Grand Rapida: Eerdmans, 1982), 1.1. Italics by translator.
56. Augustine, *Confessions*, trans. Edward B. Pusey (New York: Random House, 1949), bk. 6.
57. Quoted by Glover, *Conflict of Religions*, 160.
58. Clement of Alexandria, *The Stromateis*, trans. James Donaldson (New York: Scribners, 1903), 3.49, 1–3.

Chapter 2: Women's Role in Marriage

1. Sometimes Paul used *arche* to refer to angelic and demonic rulers rather than earthly ones. However, he did use it for ordinary human authorities as well, as in Titus 3:1 (compare Luke 12:11), just as it is frequently used in the Septuagint.
2. This is especially evident in Judg. 11:11, where Jephthah is recruited to lead a military force against the Ammonites. The people of Gilead, according to the Hebrew, make him both ruler (*qatsin*) and head (*rosh*) over them. The Septuagint translates this to *archegon* (ruler) and *kephale* (leader into battle).

The translators faced a special problem in two instances when *rosh* meant both "physical head" and "ruler," as in the analogy of head versus tail. In Deut. 28:13, they left *rosh* as *kephale*, in order to make sense of the wording. In Isa. 9:14–15, they first translated *rosh* as *kephale*, so the reader would understand, and then translated *rosh* the second time as *arche*, to drive home the point that leadership was being discussed.

3. H. Baltensweiler, *Die Ehe im Neuen Testament* (Zurich: Zwingli, Adhandlungen zur Theologie des Alten und Neuen Testaments), p. 219, n. 4. I am grateful to Marcus Barth, in the Anchor Bible, for this reference.
4. Quoted by Nathaniel Ausubel, *The Book of Jewish Knowledge* (New York: Crown, 1964), 155.

Chapter 3: Women's Place in the Church

1. Herodotus, *Histories*, 1.199.
2. Bullough, *Prostitution*, 20.
3. Quotation in Greek by J. C. Stobart, *The Glory that was Greece* (New York: Hawthorn, 1964), 103.
4. See Livy, *History*, trans. R.S. Conway, (New York: Oxford University Press, 1920), 10.31; and Juvenal, *Satire*, trans. Jerome Mazzaro (Ann Arbor: University of Michigan, 1965), 9.24,27.
5. Mishnah, *Ketuboth* 7:6.
6. Mishnah, *Nashim* 1:8.
7. Talmud, *Meg.* 23a.
8. Chrysostom, trans. *Nicene and Post-Nicene Fathers* (Grand Rapids: Eerdmans, 1956), 11.554, 13.515.
9. Chrysostom, *ibid. title*, 11.550.
10. Ibid., *11.555.*
11. Aristotle, *Politics*, trans. *Benjamin Jowett (New York: Walter J. Black, 1943)*, 1.13.
12. J. B. Phillips's translation, as well as the New English Bible.
13. Kari Torjesen Malcolm, *Women at the Crossroads* (Downers Grove, IL: InterVarsity, 1982), 73–74.

Chapter 4: Educating Women

1. Mishnah, *Nedarim* 4:3.
2. Mishnah, *Sotah* 3:4.
3. Talmud, *Yoma* 66b.
4. Paul spoke of "all men" in verses 1 and 3, but he used the word *anthropos* (an-THROW-pos), which means "man" in terms of humanity, rather than the word *aner* (an-AIR), which means "man" (male) or "husband."
5. Mishnah, *Ketuboth* 7:6.
6. Mishnah, *Aboth* 1:5.
7. "On the Origin of the World," *The Nag Hammadi Library*, James M. Robinson, editor (San Francisco: Harper & Row, 1987) 2.5.113-16.
8. Ibid., 118-20.
9. "The Hypostasis of the Archons," *The Nag Hammadi Library* 2.4.90.20-21.; "On the Origin of the World," 2.5.119.11-13.

10. Gnostic writings avoid the longer, biblical phrase, "the tree of knowledge of good and evil."

Chapter 5: The Question of Dress and Hairstyles

1. Mishnah, *Ketuboth* 7:6.
2. Mishnah, *Sotah* 3:8.
3. Talmud, *Yoma* 47a.
4. Quoted by William Iverson, *O the Times! O the Manners!* (New York: William Morrow, 1965), 39.
5. J. H. Schmidt, *Synonymik der Griechischen Sprache*, vol. 2, p. 21, quoted in J. H. Thayer's *Greek-English Lexicon of the New Testament* (Grand Rapids, MI Zondervan, 1889), 354.
6. The other Gospel writers report the number of angels and women differently, but reference is made to Luke because he traveled with Paul, and most likely Paul's understanding of the event is best reflected in Luke's writing.

Chapter 6: Is Celibacy Holy?

1. *Yebamoth* 63a.
2. *Yebamoth* 63b.
3. *Yebamoth* 63b.
4. *Yebamoth* 64a.
5. *Yebamoth* 6:6.
6. Compare Jesus' words to the women of Jerusalem, as he was led away to be crucified, in Luke 23:27–29.
7. Mishnah, *Ketuboth* 5:7.
8. Mishnah, *Ketuboth* 5:6.
9. Aristotle, *Nicomachean Ethics*, 1162A.
10. Aristotle, *Politics*, 4.1552A, 1553B.
11. Bullough, *Prostitution*, 53.
12. Cicero, "In Defense of Caelius," trans. C.D. Yonge, *The Orations of Cicero*, vol 3 (London: Bell & Daldy, 1871), 22.
13. Quotation by Barclay, *Daily Study Bible*, vol. 12, 89.
14. Ibid., 90.
15. Ovid, "The Loves," trans. Rolfe Humphries (Bloomington: Indiana University, 1957), 4.37-38, 41-42.
16. Quotation by Barclay, *Daily Study Bible*, vol. 12, 90.
17. Juvenal, trans. Peter Green (Baltimore: Penguin, 1967), 6.52-54.
18. Quotation by Barclay, *Daily Study Bible*, vol. 12, 90.
19. Quoted by Barclay, *Daily Study Bible*, vol. 1, 155.
20. Bullough, *Prostitution*, 56.
21. *Ibid.*
22. Aulus Celsus, *De Medicina*, I 1,4., quoted by Bullogh, *Prostitution*, 57.
23. Soranus of Ephesis, *Gynecology*, trans. O.W. Temkin (Baltimore: Johns Hopkins Press, 1956), 1.7.
24. Philo, *Special Laws*, 3.113.

25. Porphyry, *Abstinence from Animal Food*, trans. Thomas Taylor (London: Thomas Rodd, 1823), 1,45; 4,8, 20, et al.
26. Mark's reference to a wife divorcing her husband has puzzled biblical scholars, since Jewish women were allowed to initiate divorce only under extremely unusual conditions, such as if their husbands became lepers, or suddenly became tanners of hides.
27. Some argue that these passages mandate that church leaders be men, and married ones at that; however, Paul simply used the masculine form of the words for these offices because he was speaking to males about polygamy. The wording is such that the emphasis lies not on the offices being filled by men, but on the mandate that the man who aspires to such an office must have *one* wife and only one.
28. Paul has been accused of carelessly granting permission for marital rape and physical abuse with these words; however, his previous declaration that our bodies "are members of Christ" (6:15) should offer a sense of the holiness and value of one's mate's physical well-being to offset such a wrongful misuse of this passage.
29. Sometimes the words are translated "the two shall become one," but in the Greek it reads, "the two shall become one flesh."

Chapter 7: The Slandered Apostle

1. Aristotle, *On the Generation of Animals*, trans. O.M. Balme (Oxford: Clarendon, 1972), 2.3.737A.
2. Aristotle, *Politics*, I.1259B.
3. Mishnah, *Yebamoth* 63a.
4. Aristotle, *Politics*, I.1254A, 1259B, 1260A.
5. Mishnah, *Ketuboth* 5:7.
6. Tertullian, *Ante-Nicene Fathers*, trans. S. Thelwall (New York: Scribner's, 1885), 4.48.
7. Clement of Alexandria, *Stromateis*, 4.58.3, 62.4.
8. Ibid., 3.68,1.
9. Quotation by Glover, *Conflict of Religions*, 160.
10. Gregory of Nyssa, *De Hom. Opif.*, XVII, as quoted by Aquinas, *Summa Theologiae*, Q. 78, art. 2. All quotations by Aquinas are from the two-volume *Basic Writings of Saint Thomas Aquinas*, ed. Anton C. Pegis (New York: Random House, 1945). "Church fathers" is a phrase coined to refer to writers in the early church and at later dates whose thoughts have deeply influenced readers through the centuries. "Church mothers" is a phrase that has not yet been coined.
11. Richard M. Pope, *The Church and Its Culture* (St. Louis: Bethany, 1965), 171.
12. Augustine, *The City of God, Nicene and Post-Nicene Fathers*, 2.281-2. The translators left this portion in Latin.
13. Ibid.
14. Such an action may seem macabre to modern minds. However, it was based on the conviction that the physical remains of an especially holy person retained a healing aura even after death, and so the parts of such a person were often cherished for centuries after his or her demise. The practice might be seen as a sort of spiritual counterpart to the modern use of the

organs of a deceased person in implanting them in a living person by surgical means in order to replace damaged or diseased organs.

15. Pope, *Church and Its Culture*, 276.
16. Aquinas *Summa*, Q. 92, art. 1.
17. Ibid.
18. Ibid.
19. Ibid., Q. 92, art. 3.
20. Ibid.
21. Ibid.
22. Ibid.
23. Quoted by Letha Scanzoni and Nancy Hardesty, *All We're Meant to Be* (Waco, TX: Word, 1974), 169.
24. Aquinas, *Summa*, Q. 93, art. 4.
25. Ibid., Q. 98, art. 2.
26. Ibid.
27. Ibid., quoting *The City of God*, 14.26. In *City*, Augustine went on to say that "intercourse would have been without prejudice to virginal integrity. For the semen could enter without the impairment of the genital organs, just as now the menstrual flow in a virgin does not impair her integrity. And just as in giving birth the mother was then relieved, not by groans of pain, but by the instigations of maturity, so in conceiving, the union was one, not of lustful desire, but of deliberate action."
28. *Letters from the Saints*, ed. a Benedictine of Stanbrook Abbey (New York: Hawthorn, 1964), 120.
29. Ibid., 78.

SUGGESTED READINGS

Kari Torjesen Malcolm, *Women at the Crossroads* (Downers Grove: InterVarsity Press, 1982).

Letha Scanzoni and Nancy Hardesty, *All We're Meant To Be* (Waco: Word Books, 1874).

Aida Besancon Spencer, *Beyond the Curse* (Nashville: Thomas Nelson, 1985).

General Index

Adam and Eve, 32, 36, 58, 113, 115; Gnostic teachings about, 74–75, 124n.10; Paul's teachings about, 44, 68–69, 83; rabbinical interpretations, 16–18, 27, 55–59

Adultery, 8, 14, 97; Jesus' teachings about, 101; Old Testament laws regarding, 22–23, 95–96, 122n.41; Paul's teachings about, 106, 111; woman accused of, brought before Jesus, 96

Alexander the Great, 11, 23, 31, 32

Angels, 87–88

Aquinas. *See* Thomas Aquinas

Aristotle, xii, 3, 8, 9, 11, 24, 25, 39, 61, 114, 117, 120n.2; marriage, views on, xii, 32, 36, 37, 43, 46, 97; women, nature of, 5–7, 9, 14, 111

Augustine, 28, 98, 113, 115, 117, 120n.2, 126n.27

Augustus Caesar, 99, 100

Authority: of women, xiii, 72, 82, 87–88, 111; in marriage, 14, 107, 116

"Be subject to" (*hupotassomai*), xi, 22, 38–41, 45, 64, 66, 71, 111, 116

Bellarmine, Robert, 118

Cato, 98

Celibacy, 26, 29, 52, 108; Augustine's teachings about, 28, 113–14; among Essenes, 24, 25, 26, 28, 29; Gnostic teachings about, 74; Jerome's teachings about, 28, 113–14; Jewish rabbinical teachings against, 93–94, 111; monastic ideal, 28, 29, 113; Paul's teachings about, 92, 106–8, 111; stoic teaching about, 8, 24, 28, 101, 107–8, 113

Celsus, 101

Chrysostom, 56, 57

Church fathers: Augustine, 28, 98, 113, 115, 117, 120n.2, 126n.27; Chrysostom, 56, 57; Clement of Alexandria, 29, 112, 120n.2; Gregory of Nyssa, 113; Jerome, 28; Tertullian, 28, 87, 112

Cicero, 97

Clement of Alexandria, 29, 112, 120n.2

Constantine, 51, 98, 113

Courtesans (*hetairai*), 7, 8, 26, 81, 97, 98; education of, 52, 89–90; status of, 52, 90

"Covet", 18–19, 21–23

Demosthenes, 7, 97

Divorce: Jesus' teachings about, 101; Jewish manner of, 53, 79, 94, 96, 101, 112; Paul's teachings about, 106, 112; Roman, prevalence of, 98–99

Education of women, xiii, 14, 83, 111; Greek attitudes about, 7, 8; Jesus' favor of, 53–54; Jewish views, 16, 20, 70; Paul's advocacy of, 70–72, 111; Roman attitudes about, 12, 14

Egyptian society, women's roles in, 9–12

Eli, sons of, 52

Epictetus, 8

Essenes: celibacy among, 24, 25, 26, 28, 29; women, attitudes about, 24, 59

Fuller, Thomas, xi, xii

Galen, 28–29

Scripture Index